Remote control

Housing associations and e-governance

Martyn Pearl and Martina Scanlon

First published in Great Britain in February 2002 by

The Policy Press
34 Tyndall's Park Road
Bristol BS8 1PY
UK

Tel no +44 (0)117 954 6800
Fax no +44 (0)117 973 7308
e-mail tpp@bristol.ac.uk
www.policypress.org.uk

British Library Cataloguing in Publication Data

A catalogue record for this book is available from the British Library

ISBN 1 86134 398 1

Martyn Pearl is Director of Housing Studies, Oxford Brookes University and **Martina Scanlon** is a consultant with Aldbourne Associates.

Cover design by Qube Design Associates, Bristol.

Printed in Great Britain by Hobbs the Printers Ltd, Southampton

Contents

Acknowledgements

The authors would like to thank Adrian Moran and Paul Spence at The Housing Corporation for their support and assistance throughout this project. We would also like to thank all of the RSL and local authority staff who were prepared to spare time to contribute to our research. Particular thanks go to Mike Yarde of London & Quadrant Housing Trust, Paul Clarke of Metropolitan Housing Trust, Chris Woods and Norman Smith of the Newham London Borough Council, Ann-Marie Guiver of Swan Housing Group and Neil Barks of Nottingham City Council, for their willingness to share their achievements in our case studies.

Martyn Pearl
Director of Housing Studies
Oxford Brookes University

Martina Scanlon
Aldbourne Associates

Executive summary

- As a whole, the RSL (registered social landlord) sector has under-performed in its exploitation of computing and information technology (CIT).
- The increase in IT investment cannot disguise a widespread lack of vision in the strategic use of technology to develop accountability and service delivery.
- There are a small number of RSLs that have emerged as exemplars in the use of technology to meet their strategic objectives.
- RSLs need to recognise the need for cultural change to fully engage with IT. At present, the majority of RSLs tend to be very process-driven.
- RSLs need to engage more with residents and stakeholders in developing an e-strategy.
- Associations need to invest more resources in training for tenants and board members; change will only occur if access to and ability to use IT is inclusive.

- RSLs need to recognise the potential of technology to both create and/or bridge the digital divide, that is, the potential exclusion from services of those without access to technology.
- There is evidence of a technology skills shortage in RSLs. This is partly a result of difficulties in the recruitment and retention of specialist IT staff to develop and maintain systems; however, it is also a gap in the skills and understanding of senior managers, housing practitioners and other support staff. This may impede RSLs in their implementation of IT plans.
- RSLs have a way to go before they are in a position to feel confident in sharing data to achieve greater transparency and accountability. Information systems remain under-developed and lack integration.
- There is still a culture among many RSLs of secrecy and ownership of information. This needs to be addressed if e-governance is to be developed.

Remote control, RSLs and e-governance

Introduction

This report examines the potential usage of information technology (IT) to enhance the effectiveness of RSLs (registered social landlords). The project on which this report is based particularly focused on examining the potential for extending the options for effective governance through remote access.

Governance relates to the dissemination of information for the purposes of information and consultation in addition to the active processes of participation and decision making.

Remote control is primarily a study about governance. This is a topic that has been located very much at the heart of government policy since the early 1990s. In its second report published in 1995, the Nolan committee, having investigated housing associations, alongside other 'local spending bodies', found them 'well-regulated and generally well-run'. In its favour, the sector has largely been prepared to recognise the need to self-regulate, with guidance being issued by the National Housing Federation (NHF) and The Housing Corporation. The effectiveness of these measures is evidenced by the relative rarity of fraud or malpractice by housing associations. However, more recently, the extent of the governance agenda has changed. Since achieving office in 1997, New Labour has embraced the governance process, not only to ensure probity, but also as key component of its modernisation agenda for the public sector, including RSLs. Thus, any examination of e-governance such as this, must consider, not only probity, but also the opportunities for promoting accountability in a much broader sense, embracing the tenets of empowerment and capacity building.

This is not solely a study about governance. It examines governance within the context of another key issue, notably technology, from which it cannot be separated. The more generalised issues relating to technofile or – phobic responses to computing and information technology (CIT) fundamentally affect an organisation's response to and ability to deliver electronic governance. When examined together they bring into sharp focus, not only the way that organisations are controlled, but their propensity for change and their vision for the future.

The implications of challenges should not be underestimated: "electronic government is nothing short of a fundamental transformation of government and governance at a scale we have not witnessed since the beginning of the industrial era" (Caldow, 1999). The approach of this report in contributing to the development of e-governance is threefold:

- Establishing the context, that is, national and international policies and practices.
- Establishing the current picture relating to RSLs and e-governance.
- Suggesting good practice and areas for future development.

This report has been written in conjunction with the production of an accompanying website, located at http://www.brookes.ac.uk/schools/planning/VirtGov.html. Many of the references and resources referred to in this printed copy are referred to further on this website.

RSLs and CIT

The role of CIT in the commercial sector has taken on a major significance in recent years. Somewhat belatedly, the UK government has also placed technology at the heart of its modernising government proposals. For social housing, CIT is a relatively recent phenomenon, particularly in the way it is now being 'rolled out' for the broadest of public consumption. Computers may have been evident in the workplace for over twenty years, but for much of that time they have been the exclusive domain of skilled professionals, senior managers and, more latterly, tools for servicing the needs of the organisational machine. This is now changing, although not necessarily as the result of a widespread innovation and vision within the housing profession.

Few RSLs appear to have adopted technology in any serious way prior to 1993/94. This reflects the much smaller scale of operation during the fair rent era, coupled with a rapid expansion during the early 1990s.

However, the last decade has seen social landlords make steady progress in recognising the potential of computers and associated peripherals to control and manipulate data. Most organisations have long established computerised systems for rent accounting and financial services. Repairs systems and the management of needs and allocations processes are other processes to benefit widely from automation. More recently, pressures for improved customer care and reductions in overheads have prompted a number of RSLs to adopt call centres as a first point of contact for tenants with routine enquiries. The impetus behind this trend is to facilitate a more effective point of access for tenants while releasing estate-based staff from more routine work to spend more time out in their patches.

The developing trend towards transparency, partnership and choice has been at the centre of the government's approach towards services in the public sector. This is further emphasised in the current Housing Policy Statement (DETR, 2000a), which strongly promotes these themes.

Yet, despite these innovations, RSLs have been relatively conservative in their implementation of new technology and in perceiving and realising its potential. CIT should undoubtedly remain a tool rather than a principal driver of services; however, the significant opportunities it offers for radical change should not be underestimated. Relatively few RSLs have developed any substantive presence on the world wide web, or made use of electronic communication other than as an internal tool. Although this situation appears slowly to be changing, there is little evidence of a shared vision about the wider applications of IT as a proactive vehicle for change rather than a passive tool. This is reflected in the Robson Rhodes survey of RSLs' use of IT:

> *The government is committed to delivering services electronically by 2005. We have assessed the extent to which RSLs are preparing for this objective but we sadly conclude that they have a very long way to go (about 98 metres in a 100-metre race). (RSM Robson Rhodes, 2000)*

This is evidenced in part by the levels of RSL investment in CIT. Although significant amounts have been spent, the indications are that for the sector as a whole, RSLs invest less in CIT than many other comparable sectors (RSM Robson Rhodes, 2000). On this basis, it is hard to see how RSLs will complete the remaining 98 metres in the foreseeable future.

The benefits of CIT

Despite the apparently bleak prospects for the early achievement of a technologically literate RSL sector, there are many good reasons for pursuing this goal.

One important factor is that the protagonists in the environment in which RSLs operate appear to be developing at a faster and more consistent rate. While this may be an over generalisation, local authorities remain under a statutory obligation to meet government targets and invest resources accordingly. This may have implications for future partnerships and collaboration.

There are also very positive reasons for RSLs to embrace technology. In striving for competitive edge, commerce and retailing have been driving an increasing level of sophistication in the use of IT. Supermarket shoppers can now access banking and insurance services while shopping for groceries; faster connections have opened up the possibility of receiving music, movies and books online. Digital TV is opening up additional new opportunities to shop and bank and interact with retailers. What might be the potential for enabling RSL tenants to pay their rent and report repairs at the same time?

Perhaps most importantly, CIT opens up new opportunities to break the mould and deliver services in ways that address key management issues, such as tenant participation, community development, consumer satisfaction, cost effectiveness and Best Value. The development of e-government could provide ways of broadening access to information and aid communication, extend consultation and facilitate discussion. It can provide more targeted and streamlined administrative and financial systems to facilitate probity and accountability. It can also more effectively collect information, views and other inputs from tenants, stakeholders and local communities.

It is hoped that this report might bring greater focus on developing a more widespread and coherent approach to the promotion of e-governance. The following chapters set out the context for this topic, together with the overall position within the RSL sector and examples of good practice that offer some direction for the future. In the Executive summary, a range of issues are identified that have implications for both the sector as a whole and for individual RSLs seeking to become more e-governance friendly. Finally, a set of recommendations is offered, which is intended to provide guidance and highlight issues that may have proved problematic in the past. In addition, a number of good practice action points are included. It is hoped that this report might provide a resource for auditing readiness for e-governance and creating an action plan for further development.

2

The context and framework for e-governance: a review of literature

Introduction

In evaluating the potential for the further development of e-governance in the RSL sector, it is important to have an understanding of the context and cultural issues that might have a bearing on such an objective. In examining the literature relating to this topic, there is an inevitable reliance on very contemporary material. The very nature of technology is located in its dynamism and rate of change. In trawling the information sources for material relating specifically to e-governance, the results become even more contemporary. This is clearly an area in its infancy. The majority of sources cited in this review refer to developments in the private or government sectors. In particular, Whitehall's modernisation of government agenda provides an important framework within which to locate this study (Cabinet Office, 1999; Office of the e-Envoy, 2000a, 2000c). However, to date, there are few sources that relate specifically to e-governance in RSLs.

The structure of this literature review is set out so as to establish the general context for the development of CIT within the UK; to examine the range of technology currently available; to make reference to the pros and cons of the strategic implementation of technology; to evaluate the current track record of public sector organisations; and to identify the issues which would be further examined through the conduct of this study.

e-democracy and governance

The main focus of this study is to examine the potential for extending the use of digital communications to enhance e-governance. To date, this appears to be a relatively little developed area in both literature and implementation. The greatest advances have been evident in the United States, where there is a growing body of literature relating to CIT and its application to the process of voting. This appears to have attained an increased head of steam following the 2000 Presidential elections.

However, despite its relative under-development, e-governance is recognised as an important element of government reform. Its potential is recognised at both national and local levels:

> There are important civic and community implications of the expansion of new technology into daily life. The Internet offers enormous potential for new channels for civic participation and dialogue ... new technologies could enable broader participation if they engage local people in issues of public concern. (LGA, Strategy and Finance Policy Review Group, 26 October 2000)

In the context of RSL governance, the expectation of greater tenant involvement is analogous to the government's wish to further enfranchise people through improved communications. In many ways, the message appears the same, "Electronic service delivery offers huge opportunities to improve public services for the benefit of citizens: more convenient, more joined-up, more responsive and more personalised" (PIU, 2000).

However, a further message runs in parallel to this vision of technological emancipation. In order to fulfil the potential of stakeholder involvement, at whatever level, organisations must critically evaluate their own abilities in this area:

If e-government is to be a tool for promoting increased dialogue with citizens and greater self-sufficiency, then the public must be given the tools with which to make informed decisions. Universal Internet access would mean that it has never been easier to promote informed debate. (Oakley, 2000, p 3)

As emphasised in the literature relating to the 'digital divide', in order for the 'technological revolution' to make any real difference, the changes may need to be radical. Changes are needed in terms of skills, knowledge and equipment for both the target service users and the organisational providers.

The context for e-governance

The current national framework for the development of CIT within the public sector has been evangelised by New Labour as part of a radical reform of government:

Citizens and consumers of government services now demand that government be more open in their dealings. Access to information and knowledge about the political process, about services and about choices available, is both a consequence, and a driver of, the information age. A more informed citizenry is in a better position to exercise its rights, and better able to carry out its responsibilities within the community. Equally, citizens as consumers expect to be involved in the process of securing services to suit their needs, to receive a higher standard of 'customer care' from government. Awareness: providing information about what will be discussed and decided, and when. Communication: developing means for exchanging views and information. Involvement: enabling opportunities for involvement in the discursive development of information and knowledge for governance. (British Council, 2000, p 1)

Since the Blair government came to power in 1997, the place of CIT on the policy agenda has become much clearer. Among the earliest pronouncements of core New Labour policy was a modernisation agenda, aimed at bringing all elements of the public sector into line with 21st century practices (Cabinet Office, 1999).

IT is revolutionising our lives, including the way we work, the way we communicate and the way we learn. The information age offers huge scope for organising government activities in new, innovative and better ways and for making life easier for the public by providing public services in integrated, imaginative and more convenient forms, such as single gateways, the Internet and digital TV (Cabinet Office, 1999).

The point made in a Local Government Association (LGA) discussion paper is that, "compared with many other countries the focus of activity on e-government in the UK has been led by central government" (LGA, 2000). Technology, in recent years, has been increasingly placed at the forefront of the policy agenda in the public sector. Its traditional uses, as a means of processing large amounts of data, or in performing standardised administrative tasks, has become even more important as the task of managing the public sector has become more complex and risk intensive. However, more recently, the potential for expanding the use of CIT as a vehicle for delivering more transparent and accountable government, and addressing social exclusion, have also been recognised.

In October 1997 the Prime Minister announced a target for government that, "within five years, a quarter of dealings with government can be done by a member of the public electronically through their telephone, TV or computer" (Blair, 1997). This programme was subsequently amended in March 2000, when Tony Blair announced that, by 2005, all government services should be available online (Cabinet Office, 2000).

In its document, *e-government* (Office of the e-Envoy, 2000a), the government sets out four guiding principles for its CIT strategy, which it relates to the whole of the public sector, including local authorities:

- building services around citizens' choices
- making government and its services more accessible
- social inclusion
- better use of information.

As with other key elements of the government's agenda for change (for example, Best Value), there is recognition that delivering such objectives is not reliant solely on process:

Implementing the strategy requires organisations to adopt coherent and compatible information policies in support of better policy making better service delivery and more efficient working. (Office of the e-Envoy, 2000a)

Cultural change is also identified as an important factor in delivering this goal. This is examined further on pages 13-14.

The nature of the technology

A range of technologies has emerged as potential vehicles for delivering the new e-government outlined below.

For many in employment and education, the development of e-mail has revolutionised communication, opening new channels both nationally and internationally. Motorola, in its annual survey of technology in the UK, indicated that 41% of PC users sent e-mails during 2000, an increase of nearly 25% on the previous year (Motorola, 2001). The limits to e-mail have, in the past, tended to be defined by access to PCs, but there is evidence of change:

Some TV-based e-mail is already appearing. This will significantly increase the number of users who could be involved in electronic voting or opinion gathering trials. (SOCITM, 2000a, p 1)

It is also widely recognised that reliance on the expansion of the home computer market at a pace similar to that of the last five years is not realistic. There are other technologies that are therefore being developed in parallel, which offer even greater opportunity for digital connectivity.

Nor is the dream of universal connectivity limited to the large national and international telecommunications corporations. Across the world there are more than 300 locations referring to themselves as digital cities, based on their efforts to fan out the benefits of new technologies as widely as possible. An example of this in the UK is Hull, which

New technologies

- Internet and Intranets
- Call centres
- Smart cards
- Public access points
- Video-conferencing
- Digital TV: the market for digital set-top boxes and digital TV units is likely to grow to 20 million in Europe by the end of 2004 (SOCITM, 2000a).
- Document management: about 50% of authorities are now using document imaging and workflow technologies, most commonly for Council Tax and Housing Benefits, but others are being developed.
- Broadband (high speed connections): "As we move to a broadband economy, we can therefore expect higher connectivity. Small businesses with a higher bandwidth connection are nearly twice as likely to trade online as their narrowband counterparts; and entirely new sorts of value added services: broadband makes possible new services not feasible over narrowband, both for consumers (eg video streaming, video conferencing, education), and for businesses (eg electronic trading communities/hubs and application service provision)" (Office of the e-Envoy, 2001).

intends, by 2005, to equip 100,000 homes and businesses with interactive TV sets that use high-capacity digital services available through telephone lines (Downer, 2001). Such proactivity promises to mitigate some of the more excluding and disadvantageous characteristics of CIT. The nature of the digital divide is examined further on pages 11-13.

To 'e' or not to 'e'

In general terms, most of the indicators relating to digital technology point to an expansion of the medium. A *Guardian* article (14 March 2001) indicated that the equivalent of 360,000 e-mail messages are sent every second in Britain, marking a 20% growth in Internet usage over a period of two months. The article went on to quote figures from the Office for National Statistics, which show 7.8

million households in Britain have Internet access, indicating a 5% increase over the previous quarter.

A further survey by NetValue in February 2001 indicated that more than 9 million homes in the UK are now connected to the Internet (NetValue, 2001), meaning that the UK's household penetration rate stands at 37.2%. The NetValue survey also found an average of 1.41 users per household, meaning that UK home Internet users number over 12 million. Over the first three months of 2000 an average of 6.5 million households in the UK could access the Internet from a home computer. That amounts to 25% of all households, and is double the number in the first three months of 1999. Also, the figures do not include new forms of access, such as digital television. The level of Internet access indicated by these statistics places the UK as one of the leading web-connected countries in Europe.

eMarketer, in its report eEurope report (eMarketer, 2001), predicts the number of active Internet users in Europe will grow from 70 million at the end of 2000, to 108 million by the end of this year, and 255 million by the end of 2004.

KPMG, in its 2001 e-government survey, found that Internet access at home or work has risen to 44%; home access is up from 29% in February 2000 to 38% in 2001; nearly two thirds of people would like to access one or more transactions online; and the main barriers to Internet usage remain access and understanding (KPMG, 2001). This, argue the authors,

> *... reveals a fundamental change in the public's understanding of the potential of electronic channels, with twice as many people now wanting to carry out online transactions (renew a passport, for example) as those simply wanting to access public service information online. (Mori website)*

There are also indications that many are finding online government a valuable resource. During March 2001, 451,000 or 3.3% of the British online population visited the Ministry of Agriculture, Food and Fisheries website, to find out information about the Foot and Mouth outbreak.

This follows the clear impetus for greater CIT within commerce and industry. Government estimates that:

- By 2004, 70% of the EU's workforce will be Internet users compared to 28% at the end of 1999, according to the International Labour Organisation.
- The European Commission expects e-commerce in Europe to grow from £17 billion at the end of 1999 to about £360 billion by 2003.
- By 2006, 90% of new jobs in the UK will require basic IT and keyboard skills (e-Minister, 2001).

Digital TV

In its most recent survey, *Consumers' use of digital TV*, October 2000, Oftel indicated a continued growth in the take-up of digital TV. Since its launch towards the end of 1998, the spread of digital TV has been rapid. By August 2000, 21% of UK homes (about 5.25 million) had digital TV, an increase of about half a million since May 2000. The profile of digital TV users has changed, with increasing numbers of older users and DE social grades. Although usage is still lower than average among these groups, generally take-up of digital TV is more evenly distributed across the population than, for example, the Internet (Oftel, 2000).

In August 2000, at least 1 in 10 digital TV customers used Internet, e-mail and online shopping, while online gaming was most popular – used by 28% of digital customers, mainly younger consumers.

Continued barriers to the take-up of digital TV include lack of interest in additional channels and programmes (34%) and the expense of equipment and subscription charges (28%). Cost remains a particular issue for the lower income groups. However, 13% of non-digital homes said they were likely to get digital TV services in the next 12 months, and it was of particular interest to the younger age groups.

A clear picture is emerging from the above data. There is an apparent consensus between service users and providers that a greater reliance of digital communication is more efficient and effective. However, while this might be an accurate reflection in part, there are some important qualifications to this positive scenario. The first relates to the ability of organisations to deliver the vision.

Implementing technology

Central government

In its second report – *Electronic service delivery* (Office of the e-Envoy, 2000b) – the government indicated the following level of achievement for all central government departments:

- 521 services to the citizen or to business were appropriate for electronic service delivery
- of these, 218 services are enabled now (42%)
- 384 services will be enabled by 2002 (73%)
- 517 services will be enabled by 2005 (>99%).

Local government

In March 2001, the DETR published two documents which outlined plans for local government online and local e-government targets (DETR, 2001a, 2001b), and introduced a requirement for every council to produce Implementing Electronic Government (IEG) statements by July 2001 (DETR, 2001b). The requirement was that each IEG should contain a combination of vision and detail, covering the following areas:

- the authority's vision for modern service delivery in 2005, incorporating an assessment of customers' needs
- identification of important cross-cutting relationships with public and private sector bodies
- overview of the anticipated costs, benefits and savings likely to accrue from seeking to meet the 2005 target
- a summary list of services with examples to be included in achieving the 100% target by 2005 and a snapshot of the current position
- a summary list of services with examples to be included in achieving the 100% target by 2005, including those which need to be joined up between tiers of local government and between local government and the wider public sector
- an assessment of those information management functions that might be done corporately, such as address management by implementing a Local Land and Property Gazetteer, in order that information is collected once and used many times
- a summary action plan with milestones of how the authority will achieve the 2005 target, essential infrastructure and critical success factors

- detail of the relationship between the IEG and the wider modernising agenda (as outlined in CLLG, 2001).

In terms of progress, a SOCITM report found the following:

In a 2000 survey of local authorities, the Society of Information Technology Managers found:

- *of 467 local authorities in the UK, 442 (95%) have websites*
- *36% of local authority websites had improved*
- *three quarters of local authorities have prepared an e-government strategy or plan to do so*
- *about 30% have appointed a senior officer as an 'e-champion' to oversee the implementation of the strategy across the authority and others plan to*
- *2% of local authorities offering council tax payments via website*
- *improved response to e-mail correspondence. (SOCITM, 2001a)*

Limited achievements

A survey from Metastorm in 2000 questioned over 50 local authorities throughout the UK (Metastorm, 2000). Almost two thirds of local governments currently believe they are below target for putting services online. Lack of budget was cited as the largest hurdle to meeting the deadlines, closely followed by lack of direction. Other problems raised include poor infrastructure, skills shortage and the difficulties posed by cultural change.

The apparent mismatch between government targets and the Metastorm survey would suggest that the quality of achievements might not be keeping pace with the level of activity. Despite the very real progress made by the public sector, there remain clear indications that technological advance is being made within relatively narrow parameters. Concerns have been voiced in a number of quarters that, culturally, local authorities and RSLs have yet to appreciate the full potential of CIT. Currently, many housing organisations perceive CIT as merely another means of delivering the same, traditional services. This is reflected in the second e-government report sponsored by Cable & Wireless:

What we know from successful (and unsuccessful) companies in the last 20 years is that simply introducing Information Communication Technologies (ICT) to a process without changing the surrounding business environment doesn't work ... e-government will have failed if the structures of government remain untouched and the processes simply get faster and easier to use. (Oakley, 2000, p 1)

The report goes on to make the point that, "too many e-government initiatives ... are about automation, not re-engineering" (p 3) with the objective being short-term savings rather than long-term benefits.

This theme is further developed in the DETR guidance for local authorities in developing IEG statements:

... they are not just about electronic service delivery (ESD) but building services around customer need to improve responsiveness and quality. This exercise is not about technology – it is about change management, continuous improvement and business transformation for the whole organisation with technology supporting the objectives ... ESD should not be viewed as an additional way to deliver services but as an essential foundation for delivering integrated, responsive and high quality services. (DETR, 2001b, p 1)

The indications are that this quantum leap from CIT strategies based on process rather than vision has yet to happen on any significant scale. This appears partly to be as the result of limitations in leadership: 'At present, understanding of the e-government proposals are not well understood by the majority of senior officers and councillors'. (Westcott, 2000)

The situation is not all bleak, but there are indications that public sector organisations are failing to understand or to reap the full benefits of CIT. The LGA make the point:

Councils and other social landlords are already developing ways in which e-mail links and Internet sites can help two-way communication with tenants ... but there are a range of other ways in which ICT could enable councils, housing associations and others to better meet the housing needs of local communities. (LGA, 2000)

These include:

- the development of local Intranets and Extranets to provide comprehensive information and advice to local people;
- coordinated entry points for logging repairs, and so on;
- comprehensive web-based information services.

RSLs

There is evidence that, as with local authorities, RSLs have taken on board the need to develop CIT in order to maintain quality and viability. As with local authorities, the core housing functions, together with finance and development, have been the primary focus of technological investment in the past. The increasing importance of performance data and information for business planning has raised the CIT profile to new levels:

RSLs have spent a lot of money procuring new housing management systems and PCs. This is reflected in relatively high IT revenue costs, increased by high depreciation values. (RSM Robson Rhodes, 2000, p 2)

This picture was also borne out by an evaluation of The Housing Corporation funding via Innovation and Good Practice Grants (IGP) for CIT projects. The report (one of the 'Big Picture' series), found that, in the four years 1996–2000, there had been over 40 projects falling into this category. The diverse range of CIT topics represented indicates a clear engagement with the wider technological issues.

This is also encouraged and driven by The Housing Corporation. As part of the machinery of government, the Corporation are themselves bound by the requirement that all services will be online by 2005. The Corporation produced an IT strategy in July 2000, and an e-business strategy in September 2000. For the year 2000/01, 570 RSLs submitted their bids for Approved Development Programme funding via the Internet as part of a pilot programme. From April 2001, the Investment Management System (IMS) will be fully electronic, enabling the submission and payment of grant claims, in addition to funding bids, and so on.

The Online Public Register of Social Landlords and the Online Registry permits RSLs to complete Section 1 of the annual Regulatory and Statistical Return (RSR) online and to update the information accordingly. Information relating to RSLs performance indicators and the Corporation's own performance assessment (PAIS) reports have also now appeared online. This is part of a clearly signalled cultural shift, in which the Corporation is expecting the Internet to become a preferred medium for conducting consultation, distribution and collection of information and promotion of open government.

However, RSLs are still struggling to obtain information from their systems at operational, management and executive levels. Not enough money is spent on IT training with, on average, £49 being spent per employee. RSLs will never maximise the benefits from their investment in systems and technology if they do not have a highly IT-skilled workforce. (RSM Robson Rhodes, 2000, p 2)

The voluntary sector

As with RSLs, voluntary sector organisations are experiencing an inexorability around the adoption of CIT. A further similarity between the sectors is the huge diversity of organisation sizes and approaches to service delivery. In 1997, the National Council for Voluntary Organisations (NCVO) and British Telecom (BT) conducted a widespread survey of organisations across the sector. The results of the survey identified a number of key issues:

- online usage within the voluntary sector is low compared to other sectors, but is set to grow;
- small voluntary organisations have the greatest need for online services but lack the IT know-how and capabilities;
- there is a need to raise awareness of the potential effectiveness of online services;
- the voluntary sector is averse to risk, but recognises the need to develop online services. (BT/NCVO, 1997)

A more recent survey was conducted in 2001 among over 200 voluntary organisations (TBC Research, 2001). The key findings were as follows:

- there is a limited appreciation among many chief executives and directors of finance of the real benefits to be derived from IT;
- only around a half of chief executives visibly help develop their organisation's IT strategy;
- there is a major CIT skills shortage across the voluntary sector;
- despite the recognition of a skills shortage, many voluntary organisation do not provide adequate training.

There are a number of very clear analogies between the voluntary sector and RSLs. In both instances there is a problem in effectively managing information. The BT/NCVO survey identified:

... many voluntary organisations ... were concerned that parts of the sector are falling seriously behind when it comes to managing information. They fear this widening gap will create a two-tier voluntary sector with organisations divided into haves (the information-rich) and have-nots (the information-poor). (BT/NCVO, 1997)

Given these discrepancies, there are a range of applications for which voluntary organisations, in general, have found the Internet particularly productive:

- *As a research tool:* accessing material from government and other relevant sites.
- *Establishing a presence on the web:* raising awareness and advertising services, and so on.
- *Communicating with volunteers and staff:* a particularly important usage when operating in dispersed environments.
- *Staff and volunteer recruitment:* some organisations have used the Internet to deliver online training and induction for new volunteers.
- *Communicating and networking* with other organisations.

Although the indications are that RSLs are more advanced than many of their counterparts in the voluntary sector, there does appear to be considerable overlap in the issues to be addressed. It might, therefore, be productive to develop a more formalised exchange of views, experience and possibly even skills between the sectors.

A cautious vision

In spite of the overall picture of the growth of the Internet, there is not a universal belief in an uninterrupted expansion of Internet usage. A programme of Economic and Social Research Council (ESRC)-funded research – 'Virtual society' – suggests that:

The current rate of expansion will not continue. Overall trends of growth in Internet usage conceal a number of underlying sub-trends, including indications that large numbers of teenagers have stopped using the Internet. An article on ZDNet UK referred to figures published by research firm Cyberdialogue, which indicated that in 1999 30 million people in the US no longer used the Internet, describing themselves as 'former users'. (Wakefield, 2000)

This retrenchment has also been evident in the world of dotcoms, which, after appearing as rising stars in the firmament, have more recently experienced much greater scepticism in the harsh reality of the commercial sector.

"New technologies tend to supplement rather than substitute for existing practices and organisations.... The realms of virtual and real are much more interrelated than we have been led to believe" (Woolgar, 2000). The 'paperless office' is used as an example of this situation, where, far from reducing paper, the effect of the Internet and electronic communication is to generate additional paper usage.

In addition to supplementing 'real world' (that is, non-virtual) activities, CIT can actually stimulate more. Examples used are of virtual museums generating greater usage of actual museums and online journals stimulating higher subscriptions for the printed versions.

"Local social context remains paramount in the successful implementation of new technologies" (Woolgar, 2000). In this way, the provision of access to the Internet will not, in itself, address the potentially exclusionary potential of technology. Access tends only to be effective where it is provided in conjunction as part of a broader programme of community development, training, and so on.

To this extent, the director of the Virtual Society project indicated,

"The effects of the internet are profoundly overblown. It will change our lives, but not half as significantly as we thought.... It is not going to substantially change the lives of the great mass of the population." (quoted in Ward, 2000)

What appears to be the case is that, for some, the Internet revolution has arrived, generating significant changes to their lifestyles and working arrangements. Technology is at the core of the globalisation of the business environment and has also made major contributions to academia and the leisure industry. For others, who are either excluded or choose to shun CIT (still the majority of the population), the picture is very different. Where technophobia is a lifestyle decision, the implications may not be too great. However, exclusion from the information superhighway can have the effect of further marginalising households and communities who may already suffer deprivation. This phenomenon has been examined in Policy Action Team (PAT) 15's report, *Closing the digital divide* (DTI, 2000).

The digital divide

The opportunity offered by CIT for greater universal connectivity has been one of the principal drivers of Internet expansion. At a macro level, it has been at the forefront of the increasing trends towards globalisation, while also offering greater access to information in micro contexts (that is, to communities or locations). The government articulates in its e-strategy a belief that CIT can positively contribute to the levelling of the factors leading to deprivation:

For people living in low-income neighbourhoods, gaining and exploiting ICT skills can lead to opportunities to participate fully in the local and national economy. (DTI, 2000, p 16)

The commitment to universality is emphasised by Tony Blair in the policy statement 'Our information age – the government's vision' (Blair, undated) in which he states, "The new opportunities of the new information age must be open to all; the many, not just the few".

However, existing research, including that quoted in the PAT15 report, indicates that such equality does not, in reality, exist. In a deprived area of Leicester, a survey revealed that only 10% of households had a computer, with only 7% having access to the Internet. However, 22% had satellite TV and 9% had cable. In Lewisham, a 1998 survey showed that 1 in 6 of social class DE had no telephone or other ICT devices. While the potential of digital information may be immense, its availability is determined by both physical access and the knowledge and skills required to use the required equipment. Similarly, a survey by KPMG in 2001 indicated that it is those living in devolved and less affluent areas who are least likely to want to access online services (KPMG, 2001). However, these might be the people who would be most targeted by RSLs and other public sector organisations to benefit from such a development.

The term 'digital divide' reflects this phenomenon, recognising that, while CIT can play a part in the alleviation of social exclusion, it can also further contribute to it:

However, despite the vision of universal networking promised by the government and by those digital cities, the current reality indicates an uneven picture of achievement across the country. On both a national and global level, we also have to deal with the very real danger of creating an underclass of citizens who can't afford to access the internet, or who simply don't want to learn how to use new technology ... people cannot be excluded from the democratic process just because they are poor, or because they don't know a mouse from a modem. (Robinson, 2000)

For public sector organisations, the digital divide presents a significant challenge, but one which is fundamental to the effective delivery of services: "Unlike online shopping or banking, e-government cannot justify itself on the basis of serving a small, affluent population" (Oakley, 2000, p 2). However, in recognising the problems of exclusion, there may be a danger that the development of technology may get mired in a confusion of purpose which dictates that advancement must be universal or not at all. In such cases, the search for inclusion is discredited (DTI, 2000).

One of the recommendations of the PAT15 report was that, "By April 2002, each deprived area should have at least one publicly accessible community-based

facility to complement any home access which is available" (DTI, 2000, p 57). This would include the extension of relatively recent initiatives such as cybercafés, telecottages, electronic village halls, public libraries, and so on. They enable Internet access for those households for whom home access may not be an option:

Diversity and innovation are needed for broad social inclusion. The variety of types of e-gateway support different routes to inclusion. These approaches are likely to attract different sections of the population and the continuing plurality of approaches is likely to ensure the widest range of users. (Liff et al, undated)

Such structured provision of Internet access can also have other benefits:

Social inclusion is not just about access to hardware. It involves learning a range of new skills in a social context. Many users ... use e-gateways not just for the availability of equipment. They also value the social environment and the support they get from staff and other users. (Liff et al, undated)

This may have particular resonance for RSLs, many of which have started installing such facilities into sheltered housing schemes and other community facilities located on their estates.

This is also reflected in an action programme resulting from the PAT15 report (DTI, 2000). In October 2000, the government launched the Wired-up Communities programme, designed to extend Internet access to the most deprived areas by installing computers in homes and schools. This involved a pilot programme in Kensington, Liverpool, that aims to provide 2,000 homes with a computer. In March 2001, the second phase pilots of the Wired-up Communities programme were announced, covering 12,000 homes in six communities across England, including East Manchester, Framlingham in Suffolk and Alston in Cumbria.

In its blueprint for modernisation, the government committed to "develop targeted strategies to ensure that all groups have proper access to information age government" (CITU, 1999). The development of such an approach would appear an essential component of the strategic planning of all public sector organisations. A few, such as the London

Borough of Brent, have already taken this on board in their e-strategy:

A key target of the Council, and of e-government, is to reduce social exclusion. Service Areas must take advantage of the opportunities that e-government provides for making their services more accessible by those who may otherwise be excluded.... To promote the use of information society facilities within the community to ensure equality of opportunity and to minimise the effects of the 'digital divide' on social inclusion. (London Borough of Brent, 2001)

This would appear to offer a useful model for others to follow.

Other examples also exist, of where successful initiatives have been introduced to address the exclusionary effects of marginalisation. One such example is the Estate Line service introduced by The Quest Trust, which enables tenants nationally to engage in dialogue about how they might further develop tenant participation. Other examples of good practice are contained in Chapter 6.

Cultural change

An iterative theme throughout many of the government's e-documents is that of the need to reappraise existing approaches to services. Not just in the processes, but in their conception. To this end, CIT is promoted as offering an appropriate vehicle for delivering such change.

Technological change also presents government with an unparalleled opportunity to transform the way the public sector does business ... to break down silo-based delivery networks and to allow citizens to interact with government whenever they choose, whether at home, at work or on the move. Over time people will increasingly find that electronic delivery provides greater convenience, responsiveness and a more personalised service than other forms of delivery. (PIU, 2000)

Put simply, the major benefit of CIT is to enhance the flow of information and promote transparency where appropriate. For many professionals, this may appear threatening. As a minimum requirement, it emphasises the need for a more focused vision of information management and control.

There are a number of publications that stress the need for organisations to recognise the cultural implications for fully developing CIT. A report funded by Cable & Wireless makes the point:

It is not enough simply to automate existing processes in the hope that some will prove more efficient or cost effective; it is the processes themselves and the organisations that deliver that have to change. (Oakley, 2000, p 7)

This sentiment is further echoed in a paper produced for the LGA:

But in too many cases councils are falling into the same trap as central government. E-government is either a bolt on extra or the provision of a conventional service in a new way. (LGA, 2000)

There is also a potential danger that those CIT targets which are adopted will be limited in vision, based on current technologies and practices rather than with the potential of future development in mind (LGA, 2000). This is a danger that is also mirrored in the apparent lack of vision of the nature and shape of housing organisations for the future:

The 21st century will see office working change to a more flexible regime, with much more fluid patterns of work, all supported by communications technology. Offices could evolve to become more like clubs – a place where people with mutual interests come together to share knowledge and information. (Grinyer, 1999, p 83)

It is this appreciation of the centrality of shared intelligence that underpins both the development of effective information cultures and the theme of this report – the extension of governance. In each of these instances, the challenge to organisations in the public sector is "ensuring that government electronic service delivery is driven by the use that citizens make of it" (PIU, 2000).

Information systems

The information revolution currently being experienced is as powerful as the revolution driven by the invention of the steam engine. Just as we would never dream of delivering a service without people, finance or property, we must now recognise that in the Information Age neither can services be delivered without the right information. (SOCITM, 2001b)

The management of information remains one of the key themes of this study. Without adequate and properly delivered information, effective governance is likely to become seriously undermined.

However, there is evidence to suggest that, within RSLs, this remains a problem, "The provision of good quality information appears to be getting worse.... There remains considerable scope for improving management information" (RSM Robson Rhodes, 2000, p 14). Information management must therefore be identified as one of the key issues requiring further examination if e-governance is to be further developed.

e-risks

There are, of course, risks that accompany the technology agenda. Most computer users have experienced frustration on more than one occasion, as technology appears not to respond appropriately to their requirements. However, concerns also exist at a structural level within organisations in such a way as to inhibit the development of technological capacity. Perhaps the most common concerns are:

- obsolescence
- technological failure
- skills shortages
- security.

Obsolescence

The market place for housing and related systems has been very fluid, with suppliers arising and disappearing each year ... finding the requirements of local authorities and associations too specialised, or the rewards not great enough. (Martin and McDonald, 1999, p 17)

Although hardware has plummeted in cost over the last decade, for most organisations, the expenditure on technology can be sizeable. However, one of the problems in the past has been a failure of communication between housing and IT professionals, resulting in systems either offering a poor fit against requirements or becoming dated through inflexibility. Although this should remain a

concern, there are indications that the previous professional divide is being bridged, with most RSLs employing staff with specific IT skills. In addition, both hardware and software have become increasingly user-friendly and adaptable.

Technological failure

The ultimate disaster in any computer system is when the hardware fails. For organisations relying on terminals to allocate dwellings, respond to consumer queries and manage contracts, such a prospect is rightly daunting. There can be no absolute guarantee against such an eventuality. However, as in other areas of risk management, most RSLs have developed disaster management responses to such an event. Data is regularly backed up and usually equipment is relatively easy to replace.

On a micro level, it is more common for software to behave erratically or for minor problems to occur within the daily operational environment. Organisations are generally appreciating the need and benefits of having dedicated support staff on site to deal with these inevitable instances speedily. Over time, as more staff become IT literate, many of the more routine support tasks can probably be conducted by users.

Skills shortages

The limited availability of appropriate CIT skills is currently a major factor inhibiting change in the area of CIT. The 1999 DTI Spectrum benchmarking study (DTI, 1999) found that 40% of the UK companies surveyed felt that their employees did not have sufficient understanding of IT. This is a problem for the existing workforce, where they have not experienced CIT in schools and training may only have been geared towards on-the-job skills. But it is also an issue for different groups within the community who may not have access to adequate training even in the current educational system. Examples of this are school pupils in areas that are poorly served in terms of CIT equipment, often in deprived areas, people with disabilities, older people, and people for whom English may not be their first language.

This is further endorsed by a survey of the chief executives of voluntary organisations conducted in

2001, which indicated that 74% felt that the lack of IT skills was a key issue for their organisations and the sector as a whole.

The government has recognised that this is an issue, issuing a consultation paper through the DTI (DTI, 2001). In it they state, "We must ensure that people can obtain the learning and skills they need to take on new challenges at work", proposing an action plan to achieve this objective.

Skills development action plan

- Support business to widen the pool of talent still further by bringing into skilled ICT employment those people facing disadvantage in the labour market, including people from ethnic minority communities, disabled people and older workers. We will work with business to introduce recruitment and retention practices that meet the needs of disadvantaged groups. We will support business efforts to create a more positive image of careers in high technology sectors that helps attract a more diverse workforce.
- Work with business to reverse the serious under-representation of women in ICT jobs. We will identify global best practice that has helped women into ICT careers in other countries with a view to creating a more positive environment in the UK.
- Enable businesses to recruit more effectively and individuals to get the right job. We will map ICT qualifications and learning programmes against career paths in ICT.
- Expand the number of advanced ICT teachers and open up new teaching opportunities to business experts.
- Ensure ICT students have the right practical skills and awareness of business. In partnership with business, we will increase the opportunities for students to gain relevant work experience.

These actions must be complemented by work in individual communities to promote ICT skills.
(DTI, 2001)

The problem of skills shortage is also recognised within the voluntary sector, where a report by the Voluntary Sector National Training Organisation (VSNTO, 2000) indicated that this was an issue of real concern to managers in voluntary organisations.

In terms of organisational progress, the problem of skills shortages may be a very real issue. At the same time, it may also offer an opportunity for RSLs to use their resources to help bridge the digital divide – "better technological skills do represent the routes out of poverty for many communities" (Oakley, 2000, p 10). The linkage between technological change and community development should therefore not be overlooked.

Security

Data security is an obvious concern to all organisations in both the public and private sectors. The 1999 Data Protection Act places responsibilities on organisations maintaining electronic data in terms of access and security. However, many of the perceived benefits of CIT also have potential security concerns. A prime example relates to the ease of sharing and disseminating information. Clearly, not all information is for general distribution; however, digital data can be difficult to restrict from those with the skills and intent to obtain it. Although there have been major advances in online security through encryption, there is evidence that many people remain wary and are reluctant to give financial or personal information over the Internet (Francis, 2000).

However, although CIT may present a slightly different range of risks than that experienced by a paper-based operation, these should be set against the benefits to be derived. Risk management is a core part of the business of all public sector organisations within the current climate, and a measured, strategic approach to technology should be safeguard enough.

Summary

As might be expected from an analysis of any situation as fluid and dynamic as CIT, there are both positive and cautionary issues to emerge from the related literature. At its most visionary:

The Internet was supposed to change everything. It was supposed to re-write the rules of business and free us from the drudgery of our daily existence. It was supposed to usher in a brave new world centred around freedom, knowledge and community.... Except that it hasn't. And even if it does, more people seem to be saying, it might not be for a long time yet. (Ward, 2000)

This quote is a useful reference point from which to evaluate technology in the public sector and its potential to deliver e-governance. From the literature, there appear to be five major points that inform this report on e-governance.

1. The use of digital technology is clearly becoming a **major conduit for communication** in both the commercial and leisure environments. While there is a need for caution to be exercised in expectations of the immediacy of technological impact, there is little doubt that CIT represents a major factor in shaping the future.

2. For technology to be an **inclusionary tool**, it is necessary to be aware of the potential for exclusion. This is not solely related to the forces of deprivation, but relates equally to skill development and training. The current skills gaps, which are evident in RSLs, but also generally across the public sector, will act as a brake on the development of a CIT culture.

3. The effective use of CIT to an optimum level is dependent on a **cultural shift** within organisations. The current indications are that too few senior managers are aware of the potential of the medium. The tendency is to perceive CIT merely as a new way of delivering existing services, rather than an opportunity to deliver more responsive, personalised and accessible services.

4. CIT needs to be delivered within a strategic framework that understands and is prepared to develop effective **information management** systems. As with technology as a whole, there are often huge gaps in organisations' information 'culture', with many staff being unaware of the need for data, how it will be used or its potential critical application for risk assessment and targeting service delivery.

5. There is clearly a need for housing organisations to adopt **radical approaches** aimed at engaging those staff, board members, residents and stakeholders who are currently not part of the 'Internet revolution', and remove barriers to their participation. Research indicates that the two major reasons for non-involvement are awareness and cost. These should therefore form the basis of future information and governance strategies.

3

Research methodology and e-mail survey results

Introduction

Having established a context for the delivery of e-governance as outlined in Chapter 2, it is important to relate this more specifically to the experience of RSLs. The following three sections cover the primary research conducted for this project to further develop the themes identified.

The methodology adopted was intended to establish a base point for RSLs and consisted of a three-level investigation. These comprised:

- A short e-mail survey of over 100 RSLs designed to establish a broad picture of e-governance. This was achieved by obtaining basic data relating to the level at which RSLs engaged with e-governance issues. The questionnaire used is contained in Appendix B.
- In-depth telephone interviews with a selected range of RSLs and local authorities, where there was prior evidence of e-governance initiatives. The findings from these interviews are detailed further in Chapter 4 of this report, with the topic guide contained in Appendix C.
- Four in-depth case studies of organisations which, from the evidence of the earlier telephone interviews, offered specific models of good practice or innovation. These comprised two RSLs and two local authorities. The findings are detailed in Chapter 5; see Appendix D for the case study questionnaire.

The rationale behind the approach outlined above was to gather data for analysis through which we would obtain a picture of RSLs' operational practice. However, employing a range of contact methods to obtain the data generated other important secondary information about organisational effectiveness in using CIT. This was particularly important for the e-mail survey, which was as illuminating in its process as in the responses received. "After all", to quote RSM Robson Rhodes, "how can you conduct an IT survey today and not use the Internet?" (RSM Robson Rhodes, 2000).

In conducting their 2000 survey of RSLs' use of IT, RSM Robson Rhodes identified problems involved in conducting their electronic survey. These included incorrect contact details and a lack of response to electronic communication. Both of these factors are critical in the development of an effective system of e-governance and RSL performance could be further evaluated through the e-mail survey.

E-mail survey

The e-mail survey form was designed to be as brief, focused and easy to complete as possible. They were targeted at specialist IT contacts who had been notified to the NHF and produced as a database in February 2001. The questionnaire was e-mailed in June 2001 to 116 contact addresses. A further reminder was sent in August 2001 to non-respondents.

Table 1: E-mail survey results

Number of dwellings	IT strategy	Board members with access to e-mail	Use of IT to distribute board papers	Initiatives to increase e-governance	Plans to extend e-governance	Recruitment problems
20	n	4 (40%)	y	n	n	
106	n	6	n	n	n	
173	IT security policy	8	E-mail for agendas and minutes	n	p	n/a
180	n	dk	n	n	n	
430	Under-developed	100%	n	n	n	
430	n	70%	n	n	n	n/a – IT outsourced
482	n	8 (57%)	n	n	n	
1,051	n	dk	n	n	n	
1,100	n	4 (31%)	n	n	r	
1,125	n	2 (1%)	n	n	r	
1,315	y	11 (75%)	n	y - e-mail circulation list for tenants	5-10 years	
1,500	y	2 (14%)	n	n	Extend e-mail consultation	
1,500	Under-developed	100%	y	n	y	y – leading to some service delivery issues
2,017	y	6 (55%)	Drafts to chair/treasurer	n	n	
2,200	y	dk	n	n	n	
2,500	n	dk	n	n	n	
3,000	y	4/5	n	n	y – Intranet/contractor connectivity	
40,00	y	50%	n	n	n	
4,000	y	9 (100%)	y	n	General interest	some
5,000	y	18 (90%)	n	Training and support for BM, including equipment; access to Intranet	n	
5,000	y	dk	some	n	n	
5,600	y	4 (20%)	some	n	n	
6,500	y	16 (80%)	y	PCs for tenant reps, chairs of committees	Increasing use of e-mail with BMs	
8,000	n	chair	n	n	Interactive website	
8,000	y	50%	n	n	y	
8,500	y	dk	n	y – electronic repairs reporting, online rent payment	possibly	
10,000	y	24 (50%)	n	p	p	y – but not currently resulting in service delivery problems
14,000	y	dk	Internally, some external	Expanding Intranet	yes – but to be developed	
15,000	y	4 (30%)	n	n	n	
28,000	y	10 (75%)	y	None specific	Increase use of electronic media	
143,229						

Notes: y = yes; n = no; dk = don't know; p = possibly; BM = board members

In the event, 21 (18%) were rejected by the servers' addresses provided, returned as unknown or answered by someone other than the original addressee. Thus, even within a relatively short space of time, information was either incorrect or out of date. If the latter were true, this would indicate a particularly high turnover of IT staff, an issue about which further questions were added to the second follow-up mailing.

Of the RSLs contacted, there were 31 responses (27%) from organisations collectively managing approximately 150,000 housing units. Of these, seven were organisations managing fewer than 1,000 dwellings, 13 managed between 1-5,000 dwellings and 11 managed 5,000+ dwellings. The summary results are contained in Table 1.

E-mail survey findings

None of the RSLs managing fewer than 1,000 dwellings had developed an IT strategy. Only one had produced a security policy. All but four of the RSLs with 1-5,000 dwellings (70%) indicated that they had developed an IT strategy, as did all RSLs with 5,000+ dwellings in management. However, in only four instances (13%) were respondents either able or prepared to electronically provide copies of their strategies. In a small number of instances, respondents refused to provide their strategies because of confidentiality. The implication is that, in most instances, the document is not available in electronic form. In either of these scenarios, there are serious implications for the implementation of e-governance.

In 10 instances (32%), RSLs indicated that they were using some form of electronic communication to enhance governance. In most cases this consisted of limited e-mail contact relating to drafts of committee papers, agendas and in some cases, minutes. Of the organisations not using any form of electronic communication, only four indicated any plans to do so in the near future.

Perhaps encouragingly, almost three quarters of RSLs indicated some knowledge of current board members who were accessible by e-mail, which, in 14 instances, amounted to 50% or more of the board. Of the eight

that had no such knowledge, seven owned more than 1,000 dwellings.

As noted above, a supplementary set of questions was included in the follow-up mailing relating to potential problems with the recruitment and retention of IT staff, as this was an issue that had arisen subsequent to the initial mailing. Of the 10 RSLs that replied, there did appear to be a consensus that this was an issue, leading, in some instances, to a direct impact on the delivery of the IT strategy and other service provision.

Overall, while the results of the survey cannot be considered absolutely conclusive, there appeared to be little indication of any widespread innovation or longer-term technology vision. Although some of the RSLs surveyed had recognised the potential of technology for improving communication, few appeared to have achieved this in a strategic rather than reactive manner. There is also a concern that, within some organisations, there remains an approach to information that is very parochial and proprietal. This tends to create a culture of introspection and control. Such an approach will not readily facilitate the government's vision for e-governance in the 21st century.

A further concern is that RSLs may be failing to respond fully to the opportunities for future development and improvements in service delivery. This is suggested at both ends of the size spectrum, where technology and automation can offer significant benefits for smaller organisations with limited staffing resources, and with larger RSLs that are more dispersed and complex. There are a number of potential reasons for this, which are examined further in subsequent chapters.

4

Current CIT usage: results of telephone survey

Introduction

A telephone survey was carried out with representatives from 22 social housing organisations (see Appendix E). The interviews were carried out over a three-month period between April and July 2001. This chapter sets out the findings from this survey.

Organisations were asked how they currently use CIT. The findings suggest that usage can be divided into three categories:

- delivery of mainstream services
- information giving
- provision of management information.

Delivery of mainstream services

Many organisations related how their various offices are linked. Many have local area networks in place to enable communication between satellite and main offices. The use of an Intranet is widespread. Officers noted that this facility coupled with the use of personal e-mail is commonplace, ensuring that remote officers have access to organisational information and have quick and responsive access to colleagues located at other offices.

CIT systems form an integral part of all the organisations' operations. All have a combination of financial, housing management and business systems in place. Examples include Oracle, First Housing, IQ Vision and Academy. A number of interviewees stressed their reliance on CIT and noted that such systems "underpin service delivery".

A key issue facing organisations is achieving system integration. In many organisations, the use and procurement of CIT systems has developed in an ad hoc and exponential manner. As such, officers reported that investment in recent years has necessarily focused on 'back office' rather than 'front office' business solutions. Having put in place the systems necessary to achieve effective business operation, organisations are now beginning to focus their attention on the customer facing 'front office'.

Ten organisations reported that they use call or contact centres in some capacity to deliver services.

A number of organisations also reported using laptops as a means of ensuring that remote workers have ease of access to the organisation and enabling them to work efficiently and effectively in a dispersed environment.

Information giving

Twenty of those organisations that took part in the survey reported that they have websites. These are used mainly to disseminate information; however, a number of organisations are moving towards providing more interactive online services. Examples of online information include organisational structures, contact details, policies, service standards, Best Value information and customer newsletters. Diagnostic repairs ordering can now be carried out on a number of websites.

The use of an Intranet allows for easy access to all internal organisational information. The Intranet hosts a number of information sources including directories, diaries, policies and job vacancies.

Provision of management information

CIT is used as a business tool. Its use is essential for managing the stock, producing monitoring reports and completing returns. Organisations reported using their Intranet as a means to disseminate and publish management information.

A number of organisations use workflow and business intelligence systems. These landlords find that, along with web-based technology, the systems improve processes and automation, ensuring that information is used efficiently and effectively.

Types of CIT

The main types of CIT used by organisations were also examined. These included:

- call and contact centres
- internal and external e-mail
- websites.

Call and contact centres

The main services delivered via call and contact centres include:

- repairs
- care alarms
- Housing Benefit and rent enquiries.

Newham London Borough Council

The primary access route at Newham London Borough Council (LBC) is through their contact centre. The contact centre delivers all front-of-office services. There is a cut-off point between front and back office services.

Tracking software is also in use. This enables customer service officers to advocate on the customer's behalf. Officers contact a proportion of all callers in order to follow up the service received and to ensure the work was done. Hence, there are two aspects: follow-up and customer satisfaction.

Telephone calls to the centre remain the preferred method of contact. There is a small growth in e-mail contact. Providing a personal touch is very important as Housing Benefit enquiries are most common and require a high level of personal contact.

Call centre technology, including the use of customer relationship management and knowledge management systems, is increasingly being used by landlord organisations. The aim is to offer a single gateway to services and to deal with as many calls as possible at the actual point of contact.

Lewisham LBC's decision to introduce a call centre was based on increasing customer empowerment, the realisation that we are living in a 24-hour society and a self-servicing culture. Other drivers included the need to save and better utilise resources and staff time. The ability to free up staff time to invest in personal contact is seen as positive for many organisations.

Hanover Housing Association operates a 24-hour call centre. They also sell this service to other organisations.

Internet and external e-mail

All organisations reported that staff have personal e-mail addresses for use both internally and externally. This practice has been commonplace for some time. The use of e-mail is increasingly the preferred and most frequent method of communication internally and with other agencies.

Organisations were also aware of the increasing propensity with which customers are using e-mail.

Websites

The majority of organisations interviewed had websites and a number have won awards for their innovation. Organisations are also aware of the need to increase access to online services.

Metropolitan Housing Trust

Metropolitan Housing Trust (MHT) has two websites – one for shared ownership and one for the MHT group, which is currently under construction. The latter site will have two themes: a corporate element, where plans and other types of corporate information are hosted, and a residents' element.

A research survey has shown that around 24% of service users have access to the Internet. It is recognised that digital TV will have an all-important role to play in the future. Awareness of 'silver surfers' is also high. Access is increasing and MHT want to be proactive.

Newham LBC

Newham LBC has a website, and it was reported that a serious amount of resources have been invested in this. All staff and members use the website. Community groups also use it but more in an information receiving capacity. The organisation is exploring more interactive elements including ordering repairs and choice-based lettings.

The website has won awards for both the internal and external elements. In terms of external audiences, other professional organisations are the most common users. There is an increasing drive to bend this usage to service consumers. It must be noted that Newham is a poor borough and access to the Internet is lower than in other more affluent areas, although access is increasing at a rapid rate.

The 'Wired-up Communities' initiative is live on one council estate. On this particular estate, the concierge has access to the Internet and e-mail. Tenants can gain access through the concierge, and can also report repairs using this method of communication.

The Council is in discussion with Sky TV, and it is hoped that all council housing with communal aerials will have cable TV in the near future.

London & Quadrant Housing Trust has also won awards for their website. This was developed in full consultation with residents and is examined in more detail as one of the case studies in Chapter 4.

Organisations are investing in web-based technology with a view to making online services more interactive. Lewisham LBC views their website as an information-disseminating tool, but they also want it to be useful.

Organisations see the value in engaging customers. A number of organisations have established online services and many others have plans to develop their websites to allow customers to fill out forms, view properties, order repairs and make payments online.

Organisations are aware of customer Internet access and use. Pavilion Housing Association reported that 20% of their customers currently have access to the Internet either at work, at home or at another source. A further 10% of Pavilion customers reported that they were likely or very likely to have access within the next 12 months. Pavilion has therefore invested in its web-based technology in the knowledge that, even though there is currently limited use of this facility by customers, they need to act to meet the anticipated growth in the future.

The benefits of increasing access to digital TV are being nurtured by a number of landlord organisations. This media was described as a "platform of interactive communication".

The drivers behind CIT usage

Organisations were asked about the main drivers behind their CIT usage. For the most part they relayed that the main internal driver is to ensure a more efficient use of resources. The use of CIT also provides an impetus for addressing targets. In terms of external factors, the e-government, e-procurement and e-commerce agendas are extremely influential. Organisations were clear that effective and efficient CIT usage is central to the success of their operations.

CIT strategies

All organisations surveyed had CIT strategies in place. These strategies are increasingly focusing on providing electronic services to customers. Lewisham LBC, for example, aims to provide interactive tenant services while increasing access and creating a socially inclusive society.

The main aims and objectives of strategies are to use CIT efficiently to improve business performance in accordance with the Best Value regime. CIT requirements are informed by business needs and are incorporated into the business planning process. Other aims and objectives cited include:

- achieving tenant and staff empowerment
- developing and enhancing skills
- improving service delivery
- increasing availability and accessibility
- making government more accessible
- improving communication and providing better information
- managing records electronically
- ensuring customer focus
- giving citizens more choice
- increasing speed of access
- reducing costs and ensuring value for money
- automating processes and increasing productivity
- streamlining business processes
- increasing standards of service.

Newham LBC

The main driver for Newham LBC is the recognition of changes in consumer behaviour. There is a desire to be seen to be at the cutting edge and to be modern. Newham want to lead in this direction. There is an overall corporate IT strategy and housing is one element of this.

A further driver is the efficiencies that accrue from the use of CIT. An information data warehouse has been created with a view to making life easier for the customer. This data warehouse stores information about any contact that a customer has with the contact centre. Any information that has been collated can be easily re-used, for example, to fill out a different form. A corporate IT team maintain the data warehouse.

The IT strategy contains linkages to customer services and is geared around the enabling communities agenda.

Touchstone Housing Association view their CIT usage as decision support systems, enabling them to look critically at who and where their clients are. Customer service is at the core of activity.

Jephson Homes Housing Association has identified all those who need information from them, the type of information required and the best ways to provide this information. Their CIT strategy sets out their implementation plans.

The majority of organisations were mindful of e-government targets. Formal linkages in the strategies to tenant participation and governance were not always clear. Officers reported that customer services are central to all activity.

Metropolitan Housing Trust

MHT's business plan equates to their strategy; this is reviewed on a three-year cycle.

The main drivers in the past 12 months have been to develop more out-of-office applications – remote access and becoming web enabled.

A business improvement plan is in place. This is almost like a 'wish list' and its existence has allowed for a more coherent approach, which meets business needs.

There are a number of themes running through these drivers. The first relates to the organisation's business systems and keeping in pace with software developments. This also encompasses remote access and connectivity. Enabling people to log on and to use e-mail, constructing the website and improving access to mainline systems have been the major tasks recently. The second thread involves the management systems. This includes verifying information and ensuring that all information is conveyed and relayed in a consistent fashion. This also involves improving out-of-office working and investing in handheld information sources for remote access.

Electronic targets link into the governance agenda.

IT staff

Interviewees were asked about identified IT staff within their organisation. Depending on the size and complexity of the organisation, the number of IT staff employed varied. For example, at North London Muslims Housing Association, the Finance Officer is also responsible for IT, and at Taunton Deane Borough Council, there is a separate IT section with approximately 20 staff.

Larger local authority landlords are increasingly employing staff who are ultimately responsible for e-government. These posts tend to be at a senior level.

Customer consultation

Organisations were asked if they had consulted tenants about CIT in any way.

A number of organisations had consulted with tenants and residents by publishing information, while others had taken a more direct approach.

Methods of consultation

As organisations begin to focus on front-end use of CIT, they are increasingly consulting with end users in order to ascertain their needs and priorities, and also to ensure effective service delivery.

Newham LBC

Newham has just embarked on some consultation about CIT and has organised a round of meetings. There are 10 community fora in place, each having a steering group. It was reported that the fora are a most valued asset. Each steering group decides about consultation priorities and methods according to the needs of their local community. As such, the consultation has had a staggered start and progress will also be spread over a period of time.

Some examples of good practice

- Tenant groups were often involved in website development. London & Quadrant is a notable example of how residents can be involved in developing and delivering a website. Residents' associations are being encouraged to set up their own websites with support from the association.
- Taunton Deane Borough Council has involved an IT User Group, which includes tenants from their Tenants' Forum, in their website development.
- Numerous organisations reported that their websites act as a conduit for information dissemination. Plans are posted on the websites and customers can access and request information. Contact details for service areas are usually also available.
- Lewisham LBC provides free Internet access at various locations across the borough including neighbourhood offices and libraries. They have held an 'up and at it day' to increase public awareness. They have also held a video conferencing event at which tenants could speak online with senior officers, including the Chief Executive. Lewisham has also carried out an online survey with residents to find out their views and opinions about the modernising agenda. This proved to be very successful with a high take-up – more than 2,000 people replied.
- Taunton Deane Borough Council also reported that the use of video conferencing is a useful tool when operating in a dispersed environment.
- Hanover Housing Association has helped to provide a cybercafé facility on one estate.
- Organisations reported using tenant satisfaction and other surveys to gather information relating to access and information needs.
- Newsletters also act as a popular method of disseminating information and raising awareness about CIT facilities.
- Swan Housing Group offers customers a reward package as part of their consultation programme.
- Metropolitan Housing Trust will be hosting a tenants' conference later this year. They plan to show examples of IT usage so that tenants can see how other organisations are using IT.

Carrick District Council

Carrick operate a separate website called 'You Choose'. This was in line with their consultation campaign about the options surrounding cabinet style government; the website includes an online voting facility.

The Council is also the lead organisation in a partnership arrangement with other agencies, which is looking at setting up a project to share information. The 'Spider' project aims to strengthen these rural partners' roles in democracy and is aided by electronic methods of communication. Partners include the councils in Cornwall, parish councillors, the Tenants' Forum, regeneration agencies and the police, among others. They will all have access to a website. The project is due to go live early next year.

The Quest Trust

'Questline' run up to 20 teleconferences for tenants and officers each month. During the conferences, a lead speaker introduces the subject and provides advice and information to participants. The chairperson keeps discussion focused and highlights good practice examples. All participants receive an information pack.

Teleconferences enable people with a mix of information, opinions and advice to discuss their views in a focused way.

Assessing CIT usage

Organisations were asked how CIT usage is assessed among the following groups:

- tenants
- staff
- members.

Tenant assessment

The majority of those organisations who have websites reported that they monitor usage. This is

carried out by examining the number of 'hits' on their site over a given period of time. As already stated there is an increasing awareness of Internet growth and tenant access and use is a growth area. The nature of call and contact centre technology allows for intelligent monitoring and use of information. Intuitive systems automatically produce monitoring reports.

Nottingham City Council plans to go live with two digital TV pilots later this year. As part of the necessity to review and monitor the projects, they will agree criteria to measure success with their partners.

Newham LBC

An annual survey reports on access to the Internet. The Council as an organisation is very interested in levels of access. All libraries and local service centres provide free access.

One of the main attractions of using CIT is the improved access it provides to services. Usage and levels of access are continually monitored. There is a constant flow of information. Website usage is monitored using a feedback sheet system. Services are continually developing. Monitoring takes place at the point of consumption and aggregate information is also collated. All this information is used to inform the development of these services and others.

Staff assessment

The majority of organisations reported that policies are in place to ensure that staff use of e-mail and the Internet is legitimate and effective. Most organisations reported that staff have personal access to the Internet. In some organisations this is limited to staff who require Internet access to carry out their job.

A key issue for a number of organisations is the need to provide remote workers, such as sheltered scheme wardens, with e-mail facilities.

Metropolitan Housing Trust sends approximately 1,500 external e-mails each week. There is a new usage policy for the Internet and e-mail in place. All staff have signed up to it.

It appears that the use of personal e-mail is now commonplace and seen to be a necessary tool for carrying out day-to-day work. As such, organisations treat the use of e-mail almost the same as telephone use in terms of monitoring and assessment.

Member assessment

Organisations treat member access in a number of different ways; some provide members with laptops, e-mail addresses and Internet access for landlord business. Others do not supply any such equipment or access but may communicate with some members via their own personal e-mail addresses if this is their preferred method of communication.

When members use landlord facilities, they are expected to work in accordance with organisational policies and procedures.

Training

Organisations were asked about the provision of training for the following groups:

- tenants
- staff
- members.

Tenant training

A number of organisations related how they provide IT training to tenants' groups. Training had centred mainly on basic applications such as Word, Publisher and the Internet, with some organisations offering accreditation.

Newham LBC

Training provision is part of Newham LBC's ongoing consultation. Training is provided for tenants' associations and this takes place in some community halls. The 'Wired-up Community' has a centre with an office and also a training room. This facility is funded using new opportunities money and some general fund contribution. A jobs club operates from the training room facility.

Lewisham LBC provides access to learning through the 'Connected Communities' initiative. Familiarisation training is provided.

North London Muslims Housing Association reported that tenant IT training had taken place, which was funded by New Deal money.

As part of their website development approach, London & Quadrant provide IT training to tenants. Tenants are encouraged to pass on their newly acquired skills and knowledge to other tenants.

A number of organisations reported that they were keen to involve older people and have installed PCs in sheltered schemes. IT training is available to residents.

Staff training

Organisations reported that staff IT training was carried out as part of the induction and appraisal process. Training is also provided when new systems are put in place.

Lewisham LBC initiated cross-training for customer services staff when their call centre went live.

Pavilion Housing Association

Pavilion Housing Association was keen to expand the use of their Intranet. They wanted to ensure that all staff could access and be knowledgeable about IT.

As well as routine training opportunities, lunchtime IT workshops have been held for staff. Staff also have access to a Learning Library and to a personal aspiration fund amounting to £100 per person per year. This money can be spent on attaining additional IT training.

Member training

Evidence of member training varied considerably among the interviewee organisations. A number of organisations reported that member training was carried out on the same basis as staff training, while others reported that no member training was undertaken.

In relation to the provision of equipment, access to e-mail and the Internet, and training, depending on the organisation, members are either treated in the same way as staff or they do not receive any of these tools. Personalities and cultural factors contribute to how members are treated.

Equipment

Organisations were asked about the provision of equipment to the following groups:

- tenants
- staff
- members.

Tenant equipment

A number of organisations provided IT equipment to tenants' groups. Kiosks had also been used to provide access at key points of contact and PCs were installed at some sheltered housing units. A small number of organisations were looking at digital TV and the benefits it could bring in terms of increasing access to services.

Staff equipment

All organisations reported they work to a 'PC on every desk' rule. It could be said that this is the case in almost all organisations. The exception, as already noted, is organisations that are endeavouring to provide IT equipment to remote workers.

Member equipment

Again, some organisations provided IT equipment to members; others reported that members have access at landlord offices.

At Newham LBC, members receive an equipment package and have agreed to communicate with officers exclusively via e-mail. The equipment package has resulted in a greater propensity to use new technologies and also has an educative element. A high level of usage has resulted.

The benefits of CIT usage

Organisations were asked about the perceived benefits of using CIT. Benefits cited centred around communication and the use of information.

Poole District Council gave a typical response in relation to the benefits of using CIT: "Communication is enhanced by being more immediate and effective. The use of CIT cuts down on paper and sends out a consistent message". Many other organisations also indicated the belief that their businesses would not function without CIT.

Metropolitan Housing Trust stressed, "there is also a need to be careful so as to ensure that all customers and service users are part of the ongoing development and to break the digital divide".

The primary benefits cited include:

- speed of communication
- ease of access to information
- cost efficiency
- more efficient service delivery in the longer term
- being open and accountable
- achieving social inclusion
- creating enhanced communities
- easier monitoring of performance indicators
- providing a more responsive service
- better control over business processes
- providing a seamless service
- providing opportunities to deliver services in different ways
- less paper
- providing access to services for longer hours
- enhanced analysis
- convenience
- improved accuracy and quality of services
- increased productivity
- better information and better use of information
- providing opportunities to access wider audiences
- enhancing skills
- being perceived as a modern and progressive organisation
- automation of work processes.

Transparency and accountability

Organisations were asked how they currently ensure transparency and accountability to the following groups:

- members
- customers
- stakeholders.

They were asked how CIT is used to achieve governance.

Local authority landlords relayed the role of their committees. RSLs noted the importance of tenant representatives on boards of management.

Members receive management information on a regular basis. Members also consider performance information. Members can receive this information in a variety of ways. As stated, a number of organisations communicate with members via e-mail.

Tenant participation structures were outlined, where tenants' groups form part of the decision-making process. Newsletters and websites are the main mechanisms through which information is disseminated to the wider customer populations. Customers also receive annual reports setting out performance information and future plans.

Organisations necessarily communicate with their regulators via e-mail. They also fill out virtual forms; however, most organisations noted that paper copies still duplicate these.

Partnership working and regular communication are vital to ensuring openness and transparency.

Future CIT plans

Organisations were asked about their plans for the future development of CIT and if these plans considered how CIT could be used to enhance governance. They were also asked if they saw any potential barriers or problems to implementing their future plans.

Future plans centred around the development of their current service delivery mechanisms, such as call and contact centres, websites and increasing access through digital TV. Most future plans focus on engaging more with the customer.

Potential problems cited include:

- insufficient resources
- aligning resources to priority projects
- bringing all staff up to speed
- time taken to train and support staff
- changing mindsets
- increasing tenant access to technology
- ensuring customers receive appropriate training
- cleaning existing data
- security
- addressing huge cultural change.

5

Case studies

Introduction

This chapter provides details of a selected number of organisations in which their approach to implementing CIT offers important pointers for good practice. In offering these case studies, it is not the intention to suggest that the organisations cited here have solved all of the problems posed by technological change. Nor are they promoted as being typical, even in their respective fields. There will be many small and medium-sized RSLs whose executive would relish the opportunity to invest the scale of resources available to their larger, resource-rich competitors. However, differences in scale or sector should not invalidate the innovations illustrated by these studies. They were chosen largely for their approach and commitment, rather than for expenditure levels.

In many areas of public and public/private sector activity, innovation and vision have become increasingly important as the environment for service delivery has changed. This is perhaps more marked in relation to CIT as the gaps between organisational development and technological capacity become ever wider.

The good practice examples identified in the case studies will not necessarily be appropriate, either in full or in part, to all RSLs. There are already too many instances when off-the-shelf solutions have proven to be costly errors. However, the motivators and drivers for change are likely to be broadly similar across the sector, offering scope for sharing ideas and strategic responses.

London & Quadrant Housing Trust

London & Quadrant Housing Trust (L&Q) own and manage over 20,000 homes in a wide geographical area across South East England, but mostly in Greater London. In total, they work in 63 local authority areas, including three quarters of the London boroughs.

The association employs the full-time equivalent of 800 staff and has an annual turnover approaching £100 million. For the year 2000/01 they received in excess of £28 million in capital grants from The Housing Corporation.

Clearly, L&Q are one of the larger and more active RSLs. However, they were chosen as a case study for this report more because of the approach and innovation demonstrated by the organisation than because of their ability to invest large sums of money into technological development.

L&Q have been 'technology active' (that is, actively committed) since about 1997. Prior to this time, there was little systematic use of computers. However, there has subsequently been a clear recognition that the use of technology offers the organisation the opportunity to implement its policies, with particular reference to its ethos of tenant empowerment and community development.

Senior staff believe that L&Q has moved to a position where CIT is at the cornerstone of its strategy for the next five years. Its use is intended to improve processes and automation, and enhance business management through the use of workflow and business intelligence systems. It is expected that the use of web-based technology will improve flexibility and enable L&Q to deliver services more effectively.

L&Q have developed a three-year CIT strategy, through which they have invested resources at an annual level representing approximately 1.5% of turnover, equivalent to almost £2million per annum, including staffing costs. In addition to this, a further sum of approximately £2million has been identified for specific project costs. There is a separate IT department comprising 15 staff located at the head office. Monitoring of the information strategy is undertaken by an information strategy working group, comprising two board members, one regional committee member and members of the executive, which has delegated authority from the main Board of L&Q.

There is an unequivocal view among senior management in the association that the level of committed investment is based on a costed business rationale, and that the association and its residents will benefit by the returns achieved.

These benefits are projected on a number of fronts:

- *Improved service delivery:* automation of mechanical and repetitive processes.
- *Better communications* both within the association and with tenants and other stakeholders.
- *Cost savings* in terms of less paper usage, printing, space savings, better use of staff time.
- *Better use of business intelligence and performance data* enabling greater focus on delivering services to required standards.

The development of the IT strategy has revolved around five specific elements:

1. Development of an Intranet to serve the whole organisation.
2. Development of a document management system.
3. Development of a call centre.
4. Development of an Internet presence.
5. Development of a digital television network.

The Intranet is now in place with all staff having PCs. All permanent staff members have access to the Intranet and the Internet, with temporary staff gaining access after a set period of employment. All Internet usage is centrally monitored, but staff are allowed personal use outside the core office hours of 9am-5pm. Organisation-wide use of e-mail was introduced in 1998, and there are established policies set down for usage of both e-mail and the Internet. The Chair of the Board has been provided with a PC and an e-mail address specifically for L&Q business use. Other board members use their own, individual e-mail accounts on a more ad hoc basis.

All staff receive training in the standard software packages used by the association. L&Q maintain an in-house training department, with a full-time trainer and an equipped IT suite. External trainers are also used to supplement this resource, which is used, not only for staff, but also to provide training for tenants and board members.

The Intranet has three streams:

1. Direct access to policies and procedures, guidance, maps, standing orders (no paper copies) and so on.
2. A live news area, archived after two weeks.
3. Automation, where forms can be filled out, processed and routed.

Call centres dealing with maintenance reporting are in operation in each of the regional offices. Repairs reporting accounts for almost 60% of calls into the association.

The L&Q website was developed in full consultation with a residents panel. It was an initiative that developed following the association winning a communications award for its tenants' newsletter. The Housing Corporation provided £65,000 Innovation and Good Practice (IGP) funding for L&Q to develop resident communication further in new and innovative ways. The result was the proposal for a tenants' website.

Focus groups were carried out prior to the implementation stage of website development. The association also recruited a young technology graduate to assist them in developing their ideas to a point when they might be presented to consultants to be translated into web pages. Badged as 'Residents Online', the project was launched in 1999 to:

*   provide a resident-focused website;
*   enable access to computers in the community;
*   provide training for residents in computer skills.

Usage is monitored and at least 2,000 people visit the website each week. It was recognised in setting up the service that the number of residents in possession of or with access to computers was relatively limited – estimated at approximately 3%. However, this is expected to rise to around 30% in five years. Market research was carried out prior to implementing this initiative. An Internet steering group was established which comprises tenants and officers, which meets twice yearly.

The newsletter, *Homelife*, remains an important means of communication between the association and its tenants. It includes an article at least quarterly setting out information about the website (for example, 'How to report a repair'). Although repairs reporting online currently has a relatively low usage, it is predicted to increase in the future. L&Q aims to improve access and provide further training as part of their commitment to adult learning and community development.

This latter theme has been a major area of focus by L&Q. Driven by the association's commitment to tenant consultation and empowerment, the period since 1999 has seen significant investment in the provision of training and support facilities. However, although the association has made commitment in terms of time and culturally sensitive practices, much of the funding for this provision has come by way of external grants. In addition to the IGP funding for the website start-up costs, a further £65,000 was obtained as an Adult Community Learning Fund grant, from the Department for Education and Skills. The grant covered an 18-month period during which L&Q undertook to train 100 people in basic Internet skills.

L&Q delivered this training by working in partnership with Lewisham College, using a network of eight laptop computers, which they were able to set up at any community access point. They were clear that attracting adults traditionally excluded from such education would not be easy. Every effort was therefore made to remove any potential barriers to their participation. Not only were sessions delivered as locally as possible, financial support was made available for travel and childcare. The programme did take considerable effort to establish, with participants needing much support and encouragement. However, the proof of the effectiveness of the approach was that the association exceeded its grant target, with 180 tenants eventually benefiting from the service.

Further funding has been more recently obtained through the New Opportunities Fund. A three-year programme of training tenants in the use of e-mail, the Internet and website design has attracted £132,000. The association has committed to training up to 150 tenants each year, but, due to the success of their earlier training, has already established a waiting list of 290 tenants.

In addition to the publicity for IT training through the association's usual channels, it also regularly uses the services of an IT bus which visits estates and offers tenants an opportunity to use computers with advice and support. The association also endeavours to get the maximum value from their training investment by using a cascade system. Thus, when residents receive Internet training, they are required to make a commitment to pass on their newly acquired skills and knowledge to at least four others.

L&Q has provided computer equipment in a number of sheltered schemes and a highly successful 'silver surfing club' has been established. The association purchases equipment from Computers for Charity and uses these to equip residents' groups. They are encouraging residents' associations to set up their own websites using links from L&Q's main site and providing staff support.

A major innovation has been the commitment to develop a digital television network for L&Q residents. This is proposed through participation in dktv ('Different Kind of TV' – an emerging initiative due to extend across London) with other early participants including the London Boroughs of Camden and Newham.

As part of the programme of future development, electronic links are being established between the association and contractors. This will enable communication to be improved, produce a more streamlined process and enable more effective monitoring of performance. This approach has already been implemented for gas services.

The association is also piloting the use of teleworking, to enable some staff to work from home, or to use mobile computers in the delivery of day-to-day services. This has already delivered benefits in terms of staff retention and flexible working arrangements.

Consideration is also being given to adopting text messaging as a way of communicating with the growing number of tenants, particularly in the younger age ranges, who own mobile telephones.

Key areas of good practice

- L&Q have implemented CIT in a strategic manner that reflects the core values the association.
- The 'Residents Online' initiative is an example of technology enabling the association to deliver a

core service in a different and enhanced way.
- The use of CIT training assists in capacity building, which contributes to social inclusion and enables L&Q to communicate with its tenants more effectively.
- The development of CIT has been tenant focused, with consultation being a core component.
- L&Q have been aware of the exclusionary potential of technology and has taken account of the needs of disabled tenants and those from black and minority ethnic communities.
- There is clear evidence of innovation throughout the association's CIT programmes. This has enabled L&Q to attract over £¼million in external funding.
- There are also indications that L&Q's approach will, over time, lead to a significant body of tenants engaging with e-governance. There is already anecdotal evidence that tenants are benefiting from the use of bulletin boards for consultation and liaison.

Metropolitan Housing Trust

MHT is the largest component of the Metropolitan Housing Group, which also comprises Metropolitan Home Ownership and Refugee Housing. The group owns in excess of 12,000 dwellings located principally in London and Nottingham. MHT employs approximately 650 staff, located at 18 different sites in three regions, North and South Thames and Nottingham. They have an annual turnover of almost £37million and received grants from The Housing Corporation for 2000/01 amounting to nearly £14million.

Unlike L&Q, MHT have been less proactive in rolling out CIT to fulfil its service objectives to tenants. Although the organisation has an active programme of community development and regeneration, their approach to CIT has been largely traditional.

The area in which MHT offers itself as an exemplar is in the development and use of management information. As indicated elsewhere in this report, e-governance is only a practical option if RSLs have credible data to distribute, in a form that makes it easily accessed. MHT has made significant progress in this area.

The organisation has been technologically active since 1993/94, from which time they have adopted a rolling three-year IT strategy. The main driver of the strategic plan is the need for the organisation to manage performance in the most effective and efficient manner.

The majority of MHT staff have access to PCs, the main exception being those based at outlying sites, such as wardens in sheltered blocks. All users have e-mail and Microsoft Windows. The main business system used is 'First Housing', the financial system is Oracle (there are plans to integrate the various Oracle systems in the future), and the management system is IQ Vision. Overall, there is a high level of integration between systems and performance data.

There is an Intranet in place that serves each of the main offices. This enables MHT to provide an effective flow of information both to and from the centre for the purpose of performance monitoring.

Managers have access to updated online performance information that is flexible enough to allow the individual manipulation of data to produce a range of operational reports. This data is also consolidated into monthly digests that form the basis of reporting to MHT's main and regional committees. Although the digests are produced in hard copy, they are also available to staff and board/committee members via either the Intranet and/or e-mail. Currently, approximately 50% of the MHT board have access to e-mail, mainly as a result of their professional activities.

An increase in the pace of technology projects resulted in the development of a Business Improvement Plan, introduced during 1999. The intention behind the plan was to establish a clear process of financial appraisal and project management for all new initiatives. This process has now been introduced across the organisation.

The current level of expenditure on CIT amounts to approximately £1.2million per annum. This includes the costs of maintaining an IT department comprising 20 staff, including a full-time staff trainer.

Training is provided to all staff within the organisation on the use of standard office-based applications, e-mail and the Internet. MHT have policies on system security and Internet usage.

At the present time MHT do not provide IT training for tenants or board members, but this is under consideration.

Externally, the main MH Group website is under construction and the home ownership subsidiary has an established presence.

Future IT development plans cover a range of initiatives:

- Piloting remote working, through laptop computers or Personal Data Assistants (PDAs). Currently, remote access to the MHT server is limited to a few senior staff.
- Introducing workflow software to develop greater control and consistency in the use of the organisation's resources.
- Integrating contractors into MHT's systems through electronic communication. The organisation is conscious, however, of the need to not disadvantage smaller, local companies with which they conduct business. This strategy may, over time lead to changes in structures and processes within the organisation.
- Involve tenants more, through training and extending access to MHT's systems. A recent MORI survey indicated that 24% of the Trust's tenants had PCs, 20% had access to the Internet and 51% owned mobile telephones.

Key areas of good practice

- MHT has developed a robust strategic approach to CIT that reflects an appreciation of the need to manage and distribute data.
- Systems are generally well integrated and comprehensive performance data is produced in a regular and accessible manner.
- Data is distributed widely through the use of the organisation's Intranet and e-mail.

Nottingham City Council

Nottingham City Council owns and manages approximately 35,000 properties and has 18 local housing offices across the city. The Housing Department employs around 650 staff.

Revenue expenditure within the Housing Department during 2000/01 amounted to £122.8million; income for the same period totalled £119.9million.

A key value of Nottingham City Council is to 'put our customers first'. The aim is to make services more accessible and to improve customer contact points. The overall housing strategy states that IT will be used to improve response times and to find new ways of delivering services to customers.

CIT development in the past has focused on ensuring that all office-based staff have PCs and internal e-mail. This aim has been achieved and has brought about many improvements for staff in terms of communication and the effective use of time and resources. Future focus will be directed towards service delivery and customer-facing activities.

The IT strategy is currently being re-written. The draft strategy has moved on from focusing on staff to focusing on service delivery. Future direction is aimed at completing system integration and developing web-based technology.

There are two strands to the strategy – the corporate and departmental elements. Departmentally, housing has access to a direct customer base as they have the ability to deliver services directly to customers' homes.

The aims and objectives include the need to meet e-government targets. For any changes to the CIT or decisions about new technology there must be a clear business case and outline of the impact on service delivery. The draft strategy will go to the tenants' federation for their comments.

The main drive in the past few months has been to redesign the Internet site. There is a need to ensure that the Internet site is compatible with digital TV and kiosk technology. A more integrated approach is envisaged in which information systems, call centre and web-based technologies work alongside each other.

The Housing Department CIT budget amounts to £150,000 per annum. In line with the strategy, budget spending is being re-directed to customer facing activities. As part of the Council's drive for continual improvement in customer service and quality, the Housing Department intends to upgrade computer systems to a more flexible and responsive level and facilitate Best Value service delivery. To this end, the majority is now being spent on financing two pilot digital TV projects, systems integration both internally and externally, redesigning the website and ensuring compatibility across Internet platforms.

Five staff are responsible for IT. Budgetary spending and strategy implementation are monitored by a series of project review activities. Pilot milestones will be monitored quarterly.

The use of CIT has brought about considerable benefits for the organisation. Benefits cited include an increase in speed and an improvement in quality of service, information and communication. It is recognised that for systems to be effective, information must be kept up-to-date and timely.

The use of the Intranet is commonplace. It has brought about improved and speedier communication, and the Council now has a better-informed workforce. Remote workers have gained access to network and Intranet links. There has also been a reduction in the use of paper.

All organisational guides, policies, procedures and internal forms are available to staff through the Intranet. It also accommodates a staff news section for each department.

All staff have their own PC or have access to one. All staff have internal e-mail and most have external e-mail and usage is common practice. Correspondence with customers via e-mail is also increasing; there has been some use of e-mail training in sheltered schemes.

Tenants' groups receive training in the various software packages and accreditation is available on some courses. Some tenants' groups have access to IT equipment. A number of tenant representatives are online. Council research has indicated that around one in ten customers have access to e-mail.

Members have access to PCs. The chairs and lead officers have laptops provided by the Council. All members have access to the Internet and e-mail at Council House. Members have also received training on the use of e-mail.

Communication with members is increasingly via e-mail. An electronic newsletter is sent to members. Out of the 59 members, only seven still request this in a paper format.

All staff receive training through induction and appraisal systems. Each staff member has an individual development programme encompassing performance reviews. Training is also provided when new systems and software packages are introduced.

The Housing Department and Environmental Services jointly operate a call centre. The care alarm, emergency planning measures and out-of-hour repair services operate from this centre. This service expanded from November 2001 when a new call centre opened. This means that all repairs are reported through the call centre. E-mailed repair reports are also directed to the new call centre. The expanded call centre means that the repair service operates 24-hours a day.

Research has shown that approximately 86% of customers contact the Council electronically – the majority via telephone. As the Council has a decentralised structure, an important issue to consider for the future is centralising all services via the call centre.

The Housing Department has signed up to two pilot projects using digital TV. The Housing Department and NTL (It has been reported that Nottingham is fully cabled and that 40% of properties are NTL customers) are partnering on the projects, offering digital television facilities to approximately 3,000 homes. The first pilot, involving around 340 homes, went live in October/November 2001. NTL supplies each home with a set-top box, which is connected to the existing television set. This allows tenants and their families access to the Internet, e-mail and digital television services.

The second pilot will involve the same facilities being provided to around 2,400 homes on a rolling programme from late Autumn 2001. The facilities are being offered free of charge for the six-month duration of the pilots and if it is successful the Housing Department will consider how the facilities could be extended to all council properties by April 2005.

Throughout this project consultation with tenants has been ongoing. In the first instance a survey was carried out, followed by a door-knocking exercise. Information about the pilots has also appeared in the local press and in newsletters. Interestingly, 93% of customers on one estate had never used the Internet but 60% of this group reported that they were interested in taking part in the pilot. The door-knocking exercise was carried out to ascertain what type of services people would like to see provided.

Tenants will be able to use the following services via digital TV:

- report repairs and other requirements;
- apply for services;
- be consulted about the quality and type of services provided by the Housing Department and the Council;
- find out information about local events;
- receive local news.

The pilots will coincide with the launch of the new website. When tenants switch from television to digital there will be a prompt directing them to the Nottingham City Council website. It is also hoped that officers will also be able to support any tenants' and residents' associations in the area to develop their own community-based websites.

The pilots aim to improve service delivery. It is hoped that communication will be quicker, cheaper and more effective. It is not intended that the use of web-enabled technology should replace the personal approach where it is necessary or preferred by tenants. It should free up time to invest in personal contact.

The pilots will be monitored on a quarterly basis. The NTL system monitors usage using Geographical Information Systems, so different client groups' usage can be effectively and easily monitored. Defining success will be critical. Training for service users will be part of the package.

It was reported that there is an element of risk associated with the pilots in that increased accessibility runs the risk of increasing costs. As more customers gain easy access to services (for example, reporting repairs and complaints) this may result in an increased workload for officers.

The website is currently being reviewed and redesigned. Originally, each of the 12 council departments developed their own departmental pages, and as a result there is no consistency over the website as a whole. This issue is now being tackled and the new look website and Intranet will be consistent with dual-purpose information.

The new design for the website has been developed in consultation with tenants and focuses on tenants' priorities and information requirements. Ease of navigation is an important feature. The aim of the new site is to create a local information point online. In the future form filling and repair reporting will be easily carried out online and the new website will have links to other relevant organisations.

As part of the redesign process, the website is also being updated to ensure that it is compatible with digital TV and kiosk technology. The Council is endeavouring to achieve a more integrated approach through which information systems, call centre and web-based technologies work congruently.

The in-house systems are being replaced with integrated housing management, rent and benefit systems. The new systems will be Internet based and are due to be fully installed by April 2002. The systems will also have to consider Supporting People requirements. The aim is that by April 2002 the information management systems, all software and hardware and all databases will be compatible.

Key areas of good practice

- Nottingham has a number of information technology kiosks at popular contact points.
- As an organisation, the Council is aware of the possibilities surrounding electronic voting. Swipe cards have also been introduced in the Education Department to allow for payment of services.
- The overall approach to achieving integration and compatibility across information systems, call centre and web-based technologies is commendable.
- The digital TV pilots show foresight and innovation.

London Borough of Newham

The London Borough of Newham is a large organisation, with revenue spend of £350million, employing 6,000 staff. The organisation wants to be seen to be modern and at the cutting edge of CIT use. The main driver is the recognition of changing consumer behaviour; Newham want to lead in this direction. The Council's vision is that. by 2010, Newham will be a place in which people choose to live and work.

Newham use CIT in a variety of ways. The primary source of access for customers is through the contact centre. There is a current website, and more interactive elements including repairs and choice-based lettings are being explored. A key driver behind CIT usage is the efficiencies that accrue. London Borough of Newham consider IT to be the backbone on which other services sit.

A corporate strategy is in place, of which housing is one element. The major outcomes sought from this new strategy are greater efficiency and value for money, achievement of integration to support and enable the Council's key strategies, the achievement of an effective e-government strategy and improvement in service performance and delivery.

The strategy proposes short-term (3-6 months) tactical proposals and more strategic developments over the longer term (1-5 years). The strategy contains linkages to customer service and is geared around the enabling communities agenda.

The CIT strategy is based on e-government principles. The organisation is mindful of targets and contends that local authorities will need to re-engineer council services in order to achieve these.

The previous strategy concentrated on supporting the vision for increased customer focus and implementation of the Local Service Strategy – the development of local service centres and the corporate contact centre. Six local service centres were created initially with a view to increasing this number in time. The centres deal with 420,000 visitors a year. A Language Shop has also opened.

Newham's Local Service Strategy has enabled the Council's front office service to become more comprehensive, customer focused and responsive. Future focus is necessarily being directed towards the integration of back office systems in order to further develop the delivery of fully joined-up services that are efficient and effective.

Departmental developments and the creation of the data warehouse have enhanced the work on the customer service systems. The data warehouse has been created with a view to making life easier for the customer. It provides sophisticated cross-service, multi-sector analysis capabilities to support service development and better targeting. The powerful query tools enable rapid identification of relationships between different data sets and trend analysis.

The further development of Document Image Processing is ongoing. There still remains much potential, including the use of workflow, to reduce back office processing costs.

Newham has embarked on a programme to migrate its application systems (Council Tax, Housing Benefits, payroll and so on) from mainframe to client server technology, resulting in reduced costs, while maintaining reliability.

A new integrated Oracle based system is being implemented. This will include rents, repairs, Right to Buy, allocations, stock control, tenancy services, planned maintenance, homelessness and service charges.

The Housing Department has a budgetary IT spend amounting to £1.8million. This covers staffing, administrative support, equipment, printing, maintenance contracts, general communication, general hardware and software requirements, general PC replacements (there is a rolling programme of replacements and upgrades) and charges to the corporate centre.

A corporate purchasing policy ensures that all new hardware and software is compatible. Microsoft products are favoured, as are Oracle systems.

The CIT strategy and spending are monitored regularly through a series of reviews, which form part of a programmed process. IT will be subject to a Best Value review in the next year.

Newham aims to work as a single council unit ensuring complete departmental integration in terms of data sharing and communication.

All Council staff have a PC so that they are self-sufficient; most also have personal access to the Internet. This is seen as an employment benefit. An established induction process is in place, training needs are initially identified through this and appraisal procedures. Training is also provided when significant changes in CIT take place, for example, when new systems are introduced.

The Council's e-mail system is used extensively and has been upgraded to provide significant improvements in capacity, reliability and functionality. The system provides basic e-mail but also group scheduling, contact management, communication and collaboration. The organisation aims to promote and exploit enhanced usage. E-mail can be used to share and route information using customised forms, views and other advanced features. The Intranet is accessible from every council PC, and is the main channel through which information, communications and data sharing for council staff takes place. The telephone directory, the 'newsletter', the A-Z, corporate web systems, and departmental sites, including forms, policy documents and staff information are all on the Intranet.

All councillors receive a package, including a PC for home use and an ISDN line. Communication with councillors is almost exclusively via e-mail. The equipment package has provided for a greater propensity to use new technologies and a high level of usage has resulted. There is also an educative element to usage.

Each department has a departmental team with an identified IT manager. The remit of these teams is to provide operational support. There is also a corporate team responsible for maintaining the systems. Within Housing there are six people in the team. The IT manager is responsible to the Assistant Director.

A regime of service delivery performance management is in place. Management teams look at monthly performance indicator information and councillors have access to this information via the Intranet.

New Deal IT Services was created to serve the needs of the Council in the first instance and then the wider community. It is 49% owned by the Council and 51% owned by Integris in a partnership arrangement. Features include training, providing installation maintenance and support. It is heralded as a community ICT organisation.

The Strategy notes that increasingly, systems are being accessed via the Intranet and e-commerce facilities could be developed to exploit the Intranet and allow easier, more flexible and less costly procurement, invoicing and payments.

A development of the Intranet is the Extranet, which is an extension of the Intranet with selected external partners (such as Newham Online). This Extranet shares information but is protected from unauthorised access or misuse.

The Council website has won awards. The most common external audiences are other professional organisations, but there is an increasing drive to steer this usage to service consumers. It must be noted that Newham is a poor borough and current access to the Internet is lower than in other more affluent areas, although access is increasing at a rapid rate. An annual survey reports on local access to the Internet. The Council as an organisation is very interested in levels of access. All libraries and local service centres provide free access.

All types of council information, including the council timetable, is available on the website. Consultation materials about cabinet style governance and contact details are also posted on the site.

Future development of the website will be directed towards making it more interactive, allowing a two-way flow of information. However, officers are mindful, wherever possible, of eliminating the need for the public to complete forms and to make use of existing systems held data.

Newham.net is a portal site covering various aspects of the community. It is a website with a collection of associated themed web links and is much wider than a website. Access is enabled from a variety of sources, with access to all government agencies operating within Newham. It not only includes consumer needs but also links to sites for e-commerce.

The contact centre delivers all front of office services and is in the midst of implementation. A phased approach to implementation was adopted and, at the time of writing, it is more than two thirds of the way through. The centre handles two million calls per year.

Tracking software is in use, which enables customer service officers to ensure that calls are processed efficiently. Officers also call back a proportion of all callers in order to follow up the service received and to ensure the work was done. There are thus two aspects to this system – to follow-up work and check customer satisfaction.

Telephone calls to the centre remain the preferred method of contact although there is a small growth in e-mail contact. Providing a personal touch is very important as around 80% of enquiries are benefit related.

dktv ('Different Kind of TV') is providing a digital television service in the New Deal for Communities (NDC) area and provides access to broadband digital television and council services from the home. The Council is a key content provider to dktv, along with the London Borough of Croydon, St Pancras & Humanist Housing Association, the NHS, learndirect, H.O.M.E.S and Surestart. The service offers contractor bookings, direct access to the H.O.M.E.S database and callback facilities, and is vendor independent.

'ICT in the Community Group' has been created to better serve the needs of tenants and residents. The group meets with the ten community fora in the borough and takes on suggestions from the community.

The Council has also embarked on some consultation about CIT and has organised a round of meetings. Each community forum has a steering group that decides about consultation priorities and methods according to the needs of their local community. As such, the consultation has had a staggered start and progress will also be spread over a period of time. Customers can get involved in a variety of ways. These include via the contact centre, local service centres, website, tenant participation structures, newsletters, surveys and conferences.

In the future, the Council aims to ensure and provide for seamless ways of gaining customer feedback without being seen to gather that intelligence. Improving access and developing purchasing information are paramount to future development of CIT and governance.

The Carpenters Estate Wired Community Partnership was successful in bidding for DfEE funds, which will be used to provide online services to residents through computers and televisions. The project will test the value of such services and explore the best ways to deliver them. The plan is to provide set-top boxes and Internet connection points so that residents can use the television or a PC to access the Internet at high speeds.

A training room facility is provided as part of this project, funded using 'New Opportunities' money and some general fund contribution. A jobs club also operates from the training room facility.

Estate bases have been set up as an extension of the services available to tenants and residents, including CCTV. Seven estate bases are currently operational and there are plans to expand this number to 14.

Low-cost network links have been made to existing concierge facilities at the base of a number of tower blocks. The concierge staff are able to access e-mail and the Intranet to support their own work and can also access housing applications (such as repairs) in order to make enquiries for residents on work in progress. Staff can also access the abandoned vehicle database to log vehicles for removal and check the status of vehicles already identified.

The Council recognises that access to information and CIT is not sufficient alone to ensure social inclusion. A key element is the need to ensure that the community has access to CIT but that they also have the skills to exploit that technology. This will require an extensive training and skills development programme linking existing lifelong learning programmes and the Access to Jobs Strategy.

One of the main attractions of using CIT is the improved access it provides to services. Usage and levels of access are continually monitored; website usage is monitored using a feedback sheet system. Monitoring takes place at the point of consumption and aggregate information is also collated. All this information is used to inform the continual development of these services and others.

Key areas of good practice

- Newham has an array of initiatives in place, which promote and positively exploit the use of CIT.
- One of the terms of reference for the community fora was that it must be fun. The organisation sees this as essential in order to sustain involvement and ensure that outcomes are meaningful and representative.
- It is recognised that television culture is key to involvement now and will be more so in the

future. The key is to take services to people, especially disenfranchised groups such as young people.
- The overall approach to data and information management should be applauded, especially given its focus on customer contact, priorities and needs.

Swan Housing Group

Swan Housing Group has been in existence since 1998, operating in Essex, Hertfordshire and London. Prior to this it operated exclusively in Basildon under the banner of Basildon Community Housing Association, which now forms part of the group structure. The group overall comprises Swan Housing Association, Basildon Community Housing Association, Cygnet Housing Association (supported housing) and Pike Housing Services (non-registered subsidiary). Together, they currently own and manage almost 4,000 homes, with a further 500 in development. The group head office is located in Billericay and there is a number of housing offices spread throughout Essex.

The organisation has adopted a three-year rolling IT strategy, the content of which tends to concentrate more on operational rather than strategic issues. However, the group undoubtedly demonstrates a commitment to continued expenditure on IT and to further development of online services. Currently, Swan allocates £50,000 pa on IT capital expenditure and £100,000 on revenue expenditure.

Swan operates both Internet and Intranet sites. All 89 staff members have access to PCs, including e-mail and Internet connections. Each of the remote offices, including sheltered blocks, is also linked to the Intranet and has access to operational and management data provided through the 'Context' system together with 'IQ Objects'. The organisation has adopted an Internet policy and usage is monitored, albeit at a relatively relaxed level. Staff are encouraged to use the Internet, including personal usage outside work time (that is, at lunchtimes and before and after working hours).

The decision has been taken within the organisation to outsource much of its IT work and so it does not have a large IT technical department. They have entered into service level agreements with external companies to provide appropriate support and development services. The internal responsibility for IT was initially located with the Executive Director for Resources – a second-tier post – but has now been reallocated to the Business Support Manager – a tier lower. This is at odds with the approach taken in the other good practice case studies, where an IT 'champion' at senior management team level has been crucial in developing an organisational vision. Swan is therefore proof that such an approach can work, but success is dependent on other senior staff readily buying in to technology.

Swan has adopted a very proactive approach to electronic communication. One component of their e-strategy is to move towards a paperless office, with documents being digitised and located on a central server. This has the dual benefit of saving storage space and also enabling information to be more readily available across all of the association's offices.

This is also complemented by an acceptance of the potential benefits of flexible working arrangements. Thus, a number of senior and middle managers have been provided with the facility to work at home by connecting remotely into the main Swan server. The organisation has also purchased a number of laptop computers that staff are able to use when working away from their office location.

Another key driver for IT development has been the commitment to accountability and tenant participation and capacity building. Swan has located key organisational documents on its website, including its annual review and the minutes of board and committee meetings.

The association is also in the process of extending the facility for Internet access to all its tenants. This will be achieved through an ITV Digital package delivered through set-top boxes and keyboards provided by Swan. This approach received widespread endorsement from the residents when consulted. Swan will be proceeding with a pilot scheme for 250 tenants costing £140 per set-top box. The expectation is that this facility will then be rolled out to all other tenants over time. Swan hope to attract additional external funding to facilitate this.

The endorsement of tenants was further underpinned by estimates by the National Statistics Office that the relative costs of service users contacting organisations is £14 for personal contact, £6 for call centres and £3 via the Internet. Further to this, research indicated that approximately 20% of Swan's tenants already had Internet access, but that over 50% had had some experience of browsing on the Internet. In addition, 80% of tenants had the prerequisite scart connections available on their televisions to enable the set-top boxes to be connected.

In practice, such cost estimates may be less robust when IT facilities are provided in isolation. However, Swan received a £40,000 IGP grant to work with Cambridge Training and Development to provide a web-based learning portal aimed at developing basic skills in English and Maths. In addition, a further three-year grant of £110,000 from UK online and additional funds from the EU has also been attracted to provide a number of ICT centres across Basildon. These facilities, developed in partnership with Basildon Adult Community College, Kingsway (a local voluntary group) and Essex Libraries, will be available to enable all social housing tenants to access IT and develop appropriate skills.

Although the IT services detailed above are intended to be extended as widely as possible among Swan's residents, access, at least initially, is conditional. The provision of free set-top boxes will be subject to the criteria set down in the good tenant reward scheme. Thus, tenants must have maintained a clear rent account for at least six weeks or be keeping to negotiated agreements to pay off arrears. Additional benefits of the scheme include a cash bonus of £52 per annum and a faster response time for repairs.

In addition to the programme of IT initiatives detailed above, Swan are also in the process of implementing an online repairs service, which will include diagnostic guidance to enable accurate reporting. Once reported, the request will be sent directly through to a contractor, while simultaneously updating Swan's internal tenant record. Further extensions to web functionality will enable residents to pay rent online, view rent accounts and receive current information relating to service delivery.

Swan have recognised the need for adequate support and training to ensure that their initiatives are sustainable. They have made provision for an extensive staff training budget, including the employment of internal trainers. All staff receive IT training as part of their induction programme. Encouragement is also given for staff wishing to extend their skills further. Training for tenants is also available. The organisation manages a foyer for young people, involving the provision of a support package that includes a dedicated trainer to assist the development of skills for enhancing employability. In addition to the ICT centres mentioned above, Swan also uses their in-house trainers to offer peripatetic sessions to tenants in their own homes. This is particularly targeted at those who are unable to access other facilities because of disability or personal circumstances.

This emphasis on training has also been further developed to provide additional benefits to tenants. Swan has sought to recruit to permanent training posts for eight tenants who have successfully completed IT training courses, who are thus able to pass on their skills to other tenants. In this way, the benefits of enhanced skills and employment can be cascaded down to tenants.

Many individual members of the Board have access to PC equipment in their own right. Currently, Swan has provided eight non-tenant board and committee members with equipment and will provide further equipment where appropriate. IT training is also provided. Board papers are sent to members via personal e-mail addresses on an ad-hoc basis. A video conferencing facility has also been established to further enhance communication.

Key areas of good practice

- Swan appear to be an organisation that is keen to innovate and to embrace technological opportunities which offer benefits to the organisation and its service users.
- Swan have evolved an IT vision which offers the prospect of significant business improvements while clearly reflecting a resident focus.
- The tenants' online facility offers a comprehensive range of services via the Internet, available 24-hours a day.
- The emphasis on resident training and involvement is strongly geared towards promoting accountability and capacity building.
- The development of a scheme for providing digital television for all residents, coupled with training and support, offers added value and addresses the digital divide.
- The adoption of a system of flexible working and home working demonstrates an appreciation of the potential of IT to deliver productivity improvements and enhances the reputation of Swan as a good employer.
- The attraction of external funding for the provision of learning and training facilities demonstrates an innovative approach to service development and the ability to successfully work in partnership with other organisations to deliver community-based initiatives.

Digital television postscript

A common theme to emerge from nearly all of the good practice case studies above has been the commitment to develop a digital television resource. This joint approach reflects the evidence in Chapter 2, that television, rather than PCs offer the greatest potential for 'mass' appeal in the short term. It would also appear to indicate the existence of a strong business case for the development of such technology.

From current experience, there are two main options for RSLs seeking to develop digital television. The first is the less resource intensive approach, employed by Swan, Nottingham and also South Liverpool Housing, of providing services via the Internet through set-top boxes. This technology requires the development of specialist web resources, which can also be accessed by tenants using PCs.

The second approach is that adopted by L&Q and Newham. The development of the dktv initiative looks to present services through the television in a more native sense (as television programmes). The advantage of this approach is that users are more likely to feel comfortable in using the technology, which mirrors closely their existing experience of using a remote control handset rather than a keyboard.

Both of these options have benefits and implications. Clearly, the development of high quality television media is more expensive and time consuming than the production of web pages. dktv, which is an initiative initially sponsored by L&Q and St Pancras & Humanist Housing Association, will charge RSLs subscribing to the service on an annual basis, at an amount reflecting the services each RSL uses. These charges are designed to reflect the ability of each RSL to pay, and the number of customers for whom they provide a service. Already, the content providers using dktv services include St Pancras and Humanist Housing Association, the London Boroughs of Camden and Newham, Newham Primary Health Care NHS Trust, Surestart, learndirect and the H.O.M.E.S organisation. However, in the short term, the costs of this approach may initially be higher than the alternative.

The use of television-based Internet facilities also has benefits. Not only does it enable the focused delivery of information into tenants' homes, it can have the spin-off benefit of encouraging the use of the Internet and the wider opportunities it may offer. A major organisational benefit is that, as with the Internet, information delivered in this format can be updated easily and quickly, with relatively little cost.

What is clear in examining the approach and motivation of those organisations investing in digital TV is that they have been innovative and responsive to their tenants' needs. In most cases, these initiatives have also responded to a broader need to provide for communities that have histories of deprivation or disadvantage. As such, the development of digital television has been one part of a broader vision to provide access to information, choice and skills development as part of the process of community development and capacity building. These are therefore excellent examples of how technology can actively bridge the digital divide.

A result of this is that most of the organisations referred to have been able to access additional funds to the mainstream Social Housing Grant subsidy or rental income. In the cases of L&Q and South Liverpool, they both managed to attract funding from the New Opportunities Fund and the DfES. Swan and L&Q managed to attract Housing Corporation IGP grants in the development stages of their projects. Swan has also managed to attract European funding.

RSLs should be prepared to examine the potential of delivering services and information via the television, which is an almost universal medium. Much of the exploratory work has already been conducted – both Swan and L&Q having received Housing Corporation IGP funding to further develop the technology. Although relatively new, the use of television as a service delivery platform would appear to have the potential for an extended life span. RSLs choosing to examine this further should therefore consider the cost benefits strategically. This should take into account not only projected improvements in service delivery, but also its benefits as a vehicle for achieving cultural change and organisational development.

6

Summary and conclusions

Introduction

The focus of this project has been on the potential benefits of e-governance and on the readiness of RSLs to effectively implement it. In drawing together our findings, a rather mixed picture emerges. There are a number of very positive indicators, suggesting that RSLs have generally engaged with technology – the precursor of e-governance – in a proactive manner. In particular, a number of RSL websites are clearly among the leading exemplars of good practice. There has also been a steady growth in the numbers of RSLs developing websites, in many cases, underpinned by and located within, a broader IT strategy. The expansion of CIT-related facilities is also reflected in considerable increases in both capital and revenue expenditure on hardware and training.

However, to counterbalance this, there is little evidence that RSLs are integrating technology into their strategic and business planning processes. In the majority of cases, IT has been used to automate existing practices rather than to introduce alternatives. Nor does there appear to be systematic analysis of the effectiveness of CIT expenditure. This tends to be subsumed within wider performance monitoring regimes. This represents a rather shallow approach to technology, which is also reflected in the majority of RSL websites. Although there are exemplars, these remain few and the rest tend to be purely promotional and/or operational. In too many cases, the evidence of website content falls far short of organisations' vision statements. As the Internet is likely to be one of the major conduits through which e-governance is delivered, the prognosis is not good.

The methodology behind this research has been based on the need to assemble as much varied evidence as possible. Therefore, although the 'fieldwork' conducted in completing this project may not be absolutely conclusive, it is triangulated by other analyses. The response to the e-mail survey was below 30%, less than might normally be considered statistically significant, but the response, or lack of it, also offered further insights into the issue. In addition, the RSLs chosen for the telephone survey were identified as a result of publicised good practice in reports, journals and other professional material, rather than a more systematic trawl. Therefore, the possibility that there are other associations that have been innovative and progressive in relation to CIT cannot be discounted. However, the additional website analysis and feedback from a wide range of associated professionals support these other methodologies. Together they represent a significant body of evidence, which would indicate that the findings in this report are representative across the sector.

The picture that emerges is that RSLs generally appear relatively unprepared for e-governance. There is also little evidence that the development of e-governance frameworks is of a high strategic priority in the near future. Despite the exhortations of the government and The Housing Corporation, it is therefore unlikely that the RSLs will meet the public sector e-governance target of delivering appropriate services online by 2005.

Technology in RSLs – a cultural failing

In examining the achievements of the organisations studied in this report, there are signs of organisational responsiveness to technological opportunities. The case studies provide positive evidence of this. However, the indications are that cultural change has been more successfully achieved among local authorities than RSLs. This does not deny the fact that many local authorities have failed to respond to the government's e-strategy. However, the progress achieved across the local government sector is more significant than that achieved by RSLs. There are a number of potential reasons for this:

- Local authorities are generally larger, corporate bodies, with more extensive resources and expertise.
- Local authorities have a more focused purpose because of the government's unequivocal e-targets for the public sector.
- Local authorities may have a keener sense of developing governance and accountability because of their elected status.

None of the above would offer a universal explanation for this sectoral difference, but do indicate influences at work. There are also some indications that the progress achieved by local authorities in CIT is not continued after stock transfer. Few of the LSVT (large-scale voluntary transfer) associations, with one or two notable exceptions, had developed substantive websites (see the *Remote control* website), although this may not accurately reflect their broader response to technology. This might suggest, either that the housing function was not a driving force in technology, or that those local authorities undertaking LSVT were not at the forefront of CIT. An important lesson, however, is that RSLs are prepared to look for exemplars outside of their own sector, as many have done in benchmarking for Best Value. The most progressive have already done this, the rest should consider following this lead.

However, recognising that effective technological progress requires cultural change, what emerges from this study and is echoed across other sectors, is that technology in itself is rarely an answer to organisational problems. To allow technology to drive an organisation or the way it conducts its business is as inappropriate as having no recognition of its potential. It is a means to an end and cannot, through its introduction, overcome other operational or organisational problems that may have existed prior to its introduction. Its effectiveness may also be vulnerable to deep-seated institutional and cultural barriers to change, where they exist.

It is also wholly inappropriate for RSLs to be blind or uninterested in the potential offered by technology to provide alternative approaches for the delivery of services. At present, there appears to be either complacency and/or reticence among many RSLs to develop e-services further. This is often borne of the experience or perception that relatively low numbers of their tenants appear interested in accessing traditional services in non-traditional ways. This view may be further endorsed by concerns about the effects of the digital divide and/or that technology may have the effect of placing an artificial barrier between RSLs and their service users. While these concerns should not be taken lightly, neither should they provide an excuse for inaction. If 70% of RSL tenants show no immediate interest in electronic services, this should not disguise the fact that 30% may be persuaded to take an interest. It should be made clear that e-services are not intended to replace traditional methods, certainly in the short term, but rather to complement them. In this way, CIT can offer increased choice, rather than further restricting it.

Despite concerns about the digital divide affecting many social housing tenants, surveys among a number of RSLs have indicated levels of computer ownership and Internet access approaching 25%. Similarly, the growth in the number of households using digital TV and mobile 'phones has also been significant. Providing an increased array of service delivery methods also goes some way to address concerns that service users who are unable or choose not to use technology will be further disadvantaged.

For e-services to make substantive inroads into social housing, the onus is on RSLs to commit to developing the expertise and strategic vision to make them a success. This may relate to providing training to tenants as London & Quadrant have done or providing PCs to tenants and board members, as New Islington and Hackney HA have done. Most

Summary and conclusions

crucially, it is about delivering high quality options that respond to consumer requirements. Technology users, in the main, have become used to an increasingly high standard of production, whether on the TV, Internet or electronic games.

The evidence from this research is that the majority of RSLs fall short of providing that level of quality in their current products. This is borne out by the survey of the websites of those RSLs owning more that 5,000 dwellings (as listed in *Registered Social Landlords in 2000*, Housing Corporation, 2001a) (the full results of this are on the project website at www.brookes.ac.uk/schools/planning/Remcont/ VirtGovlinks.html). Each site was evaluated against a common set of criteria, covering content, ease of navigation, functionality, innovation, promotion of governance and recognition of disabled access. Each was then graded from one to five stars. Of the 57 RSLs examined, only 17 sites achieved three stars (satisfactory) or higher. The vast majority were either poorly designed, offered little or no substantive content or were purely promotional.

The RSLs most effective in engaging technology for the purpose of extending governance were not driven by the technology itself. As with so many other culturally driven initiatives of the last decade, such as Best Value, tenant empowerment and equal opportunities, the most effective implementation appears to be achieved by those organisations with a clear vision about what they sought to achieve through coherent and sensitive policy implementation. Three websites deserving particular mention are those belonging to London & Quadrant, Peabody and Family Housing Association. Each very clearly articulates the core values and strategic objectives of the organisation, which are borne out by the design and content.

In many other cases, websites did not wholly reflect the vision statements contained in them, appearing to be either driven by public relations considerations or routine operational needs. Also noticeable in many sites was a lack of innovation, epitomised by the continued requirement for visitors to request paper copies of key documents rather than being able to view them or download them online. These concerns were particularly but not exclusively noticeable among LSVT RSLs.

RSLs should also be more aware of the potentially damaging image that poor quality or insubstantial websites may present to the wider stakeholder community. This may become increasingly significant as competitors, partners, funders and regulators develop greater reliance on digital communication.

Barriers to e-governance

RSLs appear generally to be at a relatively early stage in their development of e-governance. This relates, not only to the technology required to deliver this service, but also to the cultural commitment required to collect and share data in a more open and accountable manner.

There are a number of potential reasons why progress in this area may have been inhibited. One major factor is the tradition and operating environment from which RSLs have emerged. For many, the past ten years has been a period of rapid growth and expansion. Change has featured highly in all aspects of work; however, this has largely been geared towards growth, competition and efficiency. Thus, many of the pre-1990 RSLs have expanded from small, relatively local organisations to £multi-million businesses virtually overnight. In parallel, CIT became elevated from a luxury to a necessity in a very short time span during the mid-1990s.

There are also other key issues that continue to act as barriers to RSLs in developing fully as technologically mature organisations. These are outlined in the box overleaf.

47

Potential barriers to technological development

- Few RSLs have cultivated a clear vision about the medium- to long-term objectives of technological investment. The majority perceives the use of CIT in respect of the structure and activities of the organisation as they currently exist.
- There are continuing problems for RSLs in getting operational staff to buy into and trust the use of CIT. Many non-technical staff or those with little personal appreciation of technology tend to be sceptical that the traditional, labour-intensive housing management tasks can be improved through such means. Others, particularly those in high pressure, front-line functions, are often concerned that automated data collection cannot adequately reflect the complexity of the task. They may also be worried that data that is not controlled will be misinterpreted and used against them.
- There remains a culture among the RSL executives that the provision of equipment and resources to board members and/or tenants is seen as a 'perk' and thus inappropriate. This has, to some extent, been reinforced by The Housing Corporation, where Schedule 1 issues have tended to be strictly interpreted. This needs to change in the future. RSLs must be prepared to recognise that investing time, resources and commitment in achieving longer-term aims are vital to their strategic health and to reflect their organisation's vision. 'Rolling out' equipment and training may be an important component in this process. This needs to be part of a more incentivised approach to improving service delivery.
- A continuing problem for RSLs in implementing CIT strategies relates to the issue of staff recruitment. It has often proved difficult to recruit and retain appropriately qualified CIT staff in competition with private sector.
- There are concerns about the integrity, security and potential misuse of electronic data. In many cases, RSLs have failed to develop effective information management systems to provide them with the necessary intelligence to run the business.

For the situation described above to change, RSLs must review their approach to CIT. This report has aimed to highlight examples of good practice to offer inspiration and provide valuable lessons. Outlined below are a number of recommendations that have emerged as a result of examining existing practice.

Recommendations for change

There is a need, across the sector, for cultural change, encompassing all levels of organisational hierarchy, but also changing and broadening the expectations of tenants and board members.

There is a need for greater vision, not driven solely by CIT, but substantially informed by it.

RSLs should identify a champion to promote CIT within their organisation. This need not be only at Executive and Director level, but should be someone with an enthusiasm for and insight into CIT issues. Critically, such an individual must be able to feed into key strategy and business planning within the organisation.

There is a need for greater transparency of information, clearly to be balanced with commercial confidentiality. RSLs should place less emphasis on controlling data.

RSLs should adopt a different approach to CIT training. Their existing capacity should also be used to train and equip tenants to develop IT skills. However, training should not be limited to enhancing technical skills, but should also extend to encouraging strategic vision.

RSLs should develop more rounded IT strategies. Details of projects, cost estimates and general principles should certainly be included. However, strategies should also articulate a vision of where the organisation wants to be as a result of such investment.

RSLs need to commit adequate capital and revenue investment to deliver their strategic objectives. However, such commitment should also be accompanied by adequate systems of evaluating the effectiveness of expenditure, set against initial objectives.

RSLs need to improve management of their data. There is often incompatibility in databases, and management information systems often fail to produce appropriate reporting mechanisms.

RSLs need to use data from tenant surveys relating to technology usage more proactively. Trends need to be identified far enough in advance to allow appropriate policy and infrastructural responses to be made.

RSLs need to be aware of the issues created by the digital divide and to adapt service delivery accordingly. However, they should also be sensitive to the potential of CIT to redress deprivation and reflect this in regeneration and community development strategies. Concern about the digital divide should not lead to technological atrophy.

RSLs need to be aware of the potential constraints imposed by an existing skills gap. CIT skills are transferable across sectors, and commercial companies are often able to offer more attractive salaries and employment packages. IT strategies should therefore avoid being too ambitious. However, associations should consider retraining existing staff where possible and/or developing in-house expertise by establishing trainee posts.

CIT has the potential to be both divisive and unifying. On the one hand, smaller RSLs may consider technology to be too expensive. This may be particularly true for employing staff with the specialist skills and experience to implement new CIT systems. However, when technology is implemented in a strategic and innovative manner, it can offer the potential for operating in a more productive and efficient manner. One example of smaller RSLs working cooperatively to overcome the problem of resources is the APEX group of black and minority ethnic associations (see their link on the *Remote control* website).

Good practice action plan

- RSLs should establish technology steering groups, involving tenants and board members to monitor and review IT strategies, or to develop such plans where they do not exist. These should include short- to medium-term implementation plans, together with costs and organisational implications. An existing model might be the Implementing Electronic Government (IEG) Plans required of local authorities (DETR, 2001b).
- RSLs should conduct an audit of their IT strategies to ensure that they reflect adequately the vision and context of technology, rather than solely relating to individual projects.
- RSLs should allocate capital and revenue funding to provide equipment and training for board members and tenants, both to extend the framework for e-governance and to support capacity building in local communities.
- RSLs should openly provide the e-mail addresses of all appropriate staff on their websites and in paper copy documents.
- RSLs should have regard in designing their Internet sites to the accessibility of web pages for people with disabilities. Guidance is available from a range of sources (see *Remote control* website, 'Other resources').
- All RSL sites should enable visitors to view and/or download key documents via the Internet.
- Smaller RSLs should consider joining with others to form a consortium to source cheaper equipment and appropriate levels of expertise.

Bibliography

Barbrook, R. (1998) 'Electronic democracy: an analysis of on-line representation', at http://ma.hrc.wmin.ac.uk/hrc/theory/electronicDemocracy.xml?id=theory.4.5.

Blair, T. (1997) Speech to the Labour Party Conference, October.

Blair, T. (undated) 'Our information age – the government's vision', at www.number-10.gov.uk.

British Council (2000) *Developments in electronic governance*, London: British Council.

BT (British Telecom)/NCVO (National Council for Voluntary Organisations) (1997) *On-line IT services needs of the voluntary sector*, at www.ncvo-vol.org.uk/.

Burt, E. and Taylor, J. (1999) 'Information and communication technologies: reshaping the voluntary sector in the information age?', at http://virtualsociety.sbs.ox.ac.uk/reports/vol.htm.

Byrne, J. (2000) 'Guidelines for building an accessible web site', www.ispn.gcal.ac.uk/accsites/accessguide.html.

Cabinet Office (1999) *Modernising government*, White Paper, Cm 4310, London: The Stationery Office, also at www.archive.official-documents.co.uk/documents.cm43/4310/4310.htm.

Cabinet Office (2000) *e-government: A strategic framework for public services in the information age*, London: Cabinet Office.

Caldow, J. (1999) 'The quest for electronic government: a defining vision', Washington, DC: Institute for Electronic Government, also at www.ieg.ibm.com/thought_leadership/egovvision.pdf.

CITU (Central Information Technology Unit) (1999) 'Central local information age concordat', at www.citu.gov.uk/publications/guidelines/cl_iag/concordat.htm.

CLLG (Central Local Liaison Group) (2001) 'E-government: local targets for electronic service delivery', February, London: DETR.

DETR (2000a) *The way forward for housing*, London: DETR.

DETR (2000b) *Information age government: Targets for local government*, London: DETR.

DETR (2001a) 'E-government: delivering local government online: milestones and resources for the 2005 target', London: DETR.

DETR (2001b) 'Guidelines for preparing implementing electronic government statements', London: DETR.

Downer, S. (2001) 'A loose connection', *New Start*, 23 February, pp 12-13.

DTI (Department for Trade and Industry) (1999) *Spectrum international benchmarking study*, London: DTI.

DTI (2000) *Closing the digital divide: Information and communication technologies in deprived areas*, Report of Policy Action Team 15, London: DTI.

DTI (2001) *Opportunity for all in a world of change*, White Paper, Cm 5052London: DTI, also at www.dti.gov.uk/opportunityforall/.

e-Minister (2001) 'Report to the Prime Minister', 2 April 2000, at www.e.envoy.gov.uk/publication/reports/pmreports/rep2apr.htm.

eMarketer (2001) *The eEurope report*, at www.eMarketer.com

EURIM (2000) 'A shock to the system – joined up electronic government', Briefing No 29, at www.eurim.org/briefings/BR29FD.html.

FITLOG (Foundation for Information Technology in Local Government) (2000) *Community governance in the information society*, London: FITLOG (see www.fitlog.com).

FITLOG (2001) *Electronic local government – A framework for action*, London: FITLOG.

FITLOG (2001) *Role models for the information age*, London: FITLOG.

Francis, C. (2000) 'Shoppers foil the virtual muggers', *Independent*, 2 April.

Grinyer, M. (1999) *Teleworking - A good practice guide*, Coventry/London: Chartered Institute of Housing/The Housing Corporation.

Housing Corporation, The (2000a) *Registered social landlords in 2000*, London: The Housing Corporation.

Housing Corporation, The (2001b) *E-business update*, Issue 1, March.

KPMG (2001) 'E-government for all: e-government survey 2001', at www.kpmgconsulting.co.uk/research/othermedia/ps_egov0401.pdf.

LGA (Local Government Association) (2000) *E-government: A revolution or business as usual?*, London: LGA.

Liff, S., Watts, P. and Stewart, F. (undated) *Inclusion in the information society: The distinctive role of e-gateways*, at the Virtual Society website, www.brunel.ac.uk/research/virtsoc/reports/Egate.pdf.

Liverpool HAT (2000) 'Liverpool HAT tenants broadcast live on the Internet', www.liverpoolhat.org.uk/internet.htm.

London Borough of Brent (2001) 'E-government strategy', London: London Borough of Brent.

Martin, A. and McDonald, A. (1999) *Buying IT*, Coventry/London: Chartered Institute of Housing/The Housing Corporation.

Metastorm (2000) '60% of local authorities confess to being below e-government targets', press release 2 November, at www.metastorm.com.

Motorola (2001) *The British and technology 2000*, Slough: Motorola.

NetValue (2001) 'US and European Internet usage', at www.netvalue.com.

Oakley, K. (2000) *E-government: Making the connection*, London: Cable & Wireless.

Office of the e-Envoy (2000a) *e-government: A strategic framework for public services in the information age*, London: Cabinet Office, at www.citu.gov.uk/ukonline.strategy.htm.

Office of the e-Envoy (2000b) *Electronic service delivery: Spring 2000 progress report*, at www.e-envoy.gov.uk/publications/.

Office of the e-Envoy (2000c) 'Framework for information age government – guidelines for UK government websites, version 2', at www.citu.gov.uk/webguidelines.htm.

Office of the e-Envoy (2001) *UK online: The broadband future*, London: Cabinet Office, also at www.e-envoy.gov.uk/publications/reports/broadband/.

Oftel (2000) *Consumers' use of digital TV: Summary of Oftel residential survey*, London: Oftel.

PIU (Performance and Innovations Unit) (2000) *E.gov: Electronic government services for the 21st century*, London: Cabinet Office, also at www.cabinet-office.gov.uk/innovation/2000/delivery/e-gov.pdf.

Robinson, G. (2000) 'From geek to glamour in 30 years', *New Statesman*, 'Generation-e' Supplement, 10 July, vol 13, issue 613, p R3, at www.newstatesman.co.uk.

RSM Robson Rhodes (2000) *Is it worth it? Survey into use of IT by Registered Social Landlords 2000*, Leeds: RSM Robson Rhodes.

SOCITM (Society of Information and Technology Management) (2000a) *The technology opportunity in year 2000 – executive briefing*, Northampton: SOCITM.

SOCITM (2000b) *So you thought it's all over – services at risk? – the growing shortages of ICT skills*, Northampton: SOCITM.

SOCITM (2001a) *Better connected 2001?: A snapshot of local authority websites*, Northampton: SOCITM.

SOCITM (2001b) *Investing in information: A detailed guide for all managers*, Northampton: SOCITM.

TBC Research (2001) *The use of information technology in non-profit making organisations*, Tate Bramauld Ltd.

VSNTO (Voluntary Sector National Training Organisation) (2000) *Skills matter: A skills foresight for the voluntary sector across England, Scotland and Wales*, London: NCVO.

Wakefield, J. (2000) 'People down mice as Internet backlash begins', *ZDNet UK*, 6 December.

Ward, M. (2000) 'The revolution will be postponed', BBC News Online, 4 December.

Westcott, B. (2000) 'Local government – trends in application of ICT', housIT, www.housit.org.uk/articles.htm.

Woolgar, S. (2000) 'Virtual society? Beyond the hype?', *The Source Public Management Journal*, at www.sourceuk.net.

Appendix A:
Relevant Internet sites

'Americans in the information age falling through the net'	http://www.ntia.doc.gov/ntiahome/digitaldivide/
BME Apex Group	http://www.bmeapexgroup.org.uk/
Centre for Civic Networking	http://www.civicnet.org/
Citizens Online	http://www.citizensonline.org.uk/intro.html
Closing the Digital Divide	http://www.pat15.org.uk
Communities Online	http://www.communities.org.uk/
Community Action Network	http://www.can-online.org.uk/
Community Information Systems Centre at University of the West of England	http://cisc.uwe.ac.uk/
Community Media Association	http://www.commedia.org.uk/
Community Web	http://www.communityweb.org/
Digital Divide Network	http://www.digitaldividenetwork.org/
E-Access Bulletin	http://www.e-accessibility.com/
E-Government Bulletin	http://www.headstar.com/egb/
EU Information Society Technologies Programme (IST)	http://www.cordis.lu/ist/
Forrester Research	http://www.forrester.com/
Foundation for Information Technology in Local Government	http://www.fitlog.com/
France in the Information Society	http://www.internet.gouv.fr/english/sommaire.html
houseIT	http://www.housit.org.uk/
Improvement and Development Agency	http://www.idea.gov.uk/
info4local.gov.uk	http://www.info4local.gov.uk/

Information Age Practice and Local Government Information House	http://www.idea-infoage.gov.uk/
Institute for Electronic Government	http://www.ieg.ibm.com
Intergovernment Technology Leadership Consortium	http://www.excelgov.org/techcon/egovex/index.htm
Liverpool HAT	http://www.liverpoolhat.org.uk/internet.htm
Local Government Association	http://www.lga.gov.uk/
London Advice Services Alliance (LASA)	http://www.lasa.org.uk/
Making the Net Work	http://www.makingthenetwork.org/
London Borough of Newham	http://www.newham.gov.uk/newmillennium/newtechnology.htm
NUA Internet Surveys	http://www.nua.net/surveys/
Office of Government Commerce	http://www.ogc.gov.uk
Office of Telecommunications and Information Applications	http://www.ntia.doc.gov/otiahome/
Office of the e-Envoy	http://www.e-envoy.gov.uk
On-Line Digital Democracy Group	http://www.ccg.leeds.ac.uk/democracy/
Performance and Innovation Unit	http://www.cabinet-office.gov.uk/innovation/
Pro Active International	http://www.proactiveinternational.com/
Quest Trust Estate Line	http://www.questtrust.co.uk/estate/default.htm
RNIB Campaign for Good Web Design	http://www.rnib.org.uk/digital/
Society of Information and Technology Management	http://www.socitm.gov.uk/
Tagish's Directory of Government Information Society Publications	http://www.tagish.co.uk/tagish/links/infosocdocs.htm
UKonline Citizens Portal	http://www.ukonline.gov.uk/
'Virtual Society?'	http://virtualsociety.sbs.ox.ac.uk/
Web Accessibility Initiative (WAI)	http://www.w3.org/wai/
Wired-GOV.net	http://www.wired-gov.net/
'Wired welfare?: the Internet support research project'	http://www.york.ac.uk/res/vcc/

Appendix B:
E-mail survey questionnaire

I am currently conducting some research for The Housing Corporation looking at the current usage and potential for developing e-governance. By this, I mean either the use of technology in the sharing of data, the conduct of the decision-making process or the involvement of stakeholders in the running of an RSL.

I would be grateful if you could spend a very short time in answering the questions below. Hopefully a report of our findings will be available within a couple of months.

My apologies if you have received this request already, and thank you for your time.
Martyn Pearl
Director of Housing Studies
Oxford Brookes University

1. Your name _____

2. Your job title _____

3. Number of dwellings in management_____

4. Do you have an IT Strategy? (If yes, is it possible to attach it to this e-mail?)

5. How many of your Board members have access to e-mail (number and %) _____

6. Do you currently use CIT to distribute board papers/minutes, etc?

7. Do you have any initiatives designed to increase the level of e-governance? If so, please describe. _____

8. Do you plan to extend the use of CIT in governance in the coming year? If so please describe. _____

9. Do you have any difficulties in recruiting and/or retaining IT staff?

If so, does this affect operational issues?   YES/NO

And/or implementing your IT strategy?   YES/NO

If so please describe._____

Thank you for your time

Appendix C:
Telephone interview topic guide

Remote control: developing CIT to enhance governance and accountability

Telephone interview topic guide

Background

This IGP funded project aims to examine the potential usage of computer and information technology (CIT) to enhance the effectiveness of RSLs. It will particularly focus on exploring the potential for extending the options to develop effective governance through remote access. Governance in this instance relates to a broad interpretation of the process, including the dissemination of material/data for the purposes of informing, updating and consulting, in addition to the more interactive processes of participation and decision making.

Purpose

To examine current practice among social landlords.

Areas to cover

1. How does the organisation currently use CIT?
   - Need to establish if they use CIT for:
     ‣ delivery of mainstream services, such as call centres
     ‣ information giving, such as a website
     ‣ management information, such as internal reports.

2. What are the drivers behind CIT usage?
   - Does the organisation have a CIT strategy? If so, could we have a copy?
   - Need to consider the aims/objectives/goals of individual CIT.
   - Strategies.
   - Need to consider how the CIT strategy is linked to others such as tenant participation, governance etc.
   - Need to consider the influence of 2005 electronic government targets.

3. What types of CIT are used?
   - Need to discuss in more detail each of the following:
     ‣ telephone, such as call/contact centres
     ‣ e-mail, internal and external
     ‣ Internet, websites – audience/usage/ information
     ‣ type/feedback methods.

4. Does the organisation have an identified IT manager? If so, at what level in the organisation?

5. Has the organisation consulted tenants about CIT in any way?

6. Does the organisation assess CIT usage among tenants/tenants' groups/staff/members?

7. Does the organisation provide any training for tenants/tenants' groups/staff/members?

8. Does the organisation provide CIT equipment for tenants/tenants' groups/staff/members?

9. How many of the organisation's members have e-mail addresses?

10. What are the perceived benefits of using CIT in the organisation?

11. How does the organisation currently ensure transparency and accountability?
- Need to consider current mechanisms in terms of:
  - members
  - tenants/customers as well as shareholding members
  - stakeholders, such as lenders, regulators.

12. Does the organisation use CIT to achieve accountability to any of the above groups? If yes, how?

13. What are the organisation's plans for the future development/use of CIT? Do these plans include training elements?

14. Has the organisation considered how CIT could be used to enhance governance? If not, why not? If yes, how and are there any potential barriers/problems?

15. Does the organisation have any good practice, innovative examples of CIT usage (teleconferencing, use of CIT in rural areas etc)?

Appendix D:
Case study questionnaire

Oxford Brookes University/Aldbourne Associates

CIT in registered social landlords questionnaire

Name of organisation _____

Interview no _____ Date _____

1. Does the organisation have a CIT strategy?
   NO ☐   YES ☐

2. Does it form part of the business planning framework?
   NO ☐   YES ☐

3. What are its main objectives?

   _____

   _____

   _____

4. What aspects of operation does it cover?

   Staff   ☐
   Tenants   ☐
   Contractors   ☐
   Board/Committee members   ☐
   Partners   ☐
   Other   ☐

5. Are there specific targets set by the policy?
   NO ☐   YES ☐

6. Are these targets monitored?
   NO ☐   YES ☐

7. Are any value-for-money criteria set?
   NO ☐   YES ☐

7a. If yes, how are these monitored?

   _____

   _____

   _____

8. Have any major changes been introduced as a result of the introduction of CIT?
   NO ☐   YES ☐

8a. Please give examples

   _____

   _____

   _____

   _____

9. What is your annual expenditure on CIT?

_____

10. Is this subdivided into specific aspects?

NO ☐   YES ☐

If yes, please give details

_____

_____

_____

11. Does your organisation have an operational Intranet?

NO ☐   YES ☐

12. Does your organisation have an operational website?

NO ☐   YES ☐

Access

13. Do all staff have access to e-mail/Internet/DIP?

NO ☐   YES ☐

14. Number/percentage of Board members, tenant representatives online

_____

14a. Do you currently correspond with these groups electronically?

Board members   NO ☐   YES ☐

Tenant representatives   NO ☐   YES ☐

15. Does your organisation use teleworking?

NO ☐   YES ☐

16. What training is offered to staff/members/service users?

_____

_____

_____

_____

_____

17. Are any services delivered online?

_____

_____

_____

_____

_____

Information

18. What management information systems are used?

_____

_____

_____

_____

19. Is management information made available to members/service users?

_____

_____

_____

_____

20. Is all of the organisation's hardware and software integrated or compatible?

NO ☐   YES ☐

20a. Are all databases integrated or compatible?

NO ☐   YES ☐

Miscellaneous

21. Do you have electronic links to other organisations?
NO ☐   YES   ☐

22. Do you have any specific CIT related initiatives?
NO ☐   YES   ☐

Any other comments

_____

_____

_____

_____

_____

_____

_____

_____

_____

_____

_____

_____

_____

_____

Appendix E:
Telephone survey –
organisation contacts

Organisation	Contact name	Address
Apex Housing Group	Andrew Evans	Spelthorne House 19–33 Thames Street Staines Middlesex TW18 4TA
Carrick District Council	Sarah Wetherill	Carrick House Pydar Street Truro Cornwall TR1 1EB
Elim Housing Association	Philip Gregory	14 High Street Thornbury South Gloucestershire BS35 2AQ
Hanover Housing Association	Jenny Williams	Hanover House 1 Bridge Close Staines Middlesex TW18 4TB
Home Group	Steve Thompson	Ridley House Regent Centre Gosforth Newcastle upon Tyne NE3 3JE
Jephson Homes Housing Association	David Jepherson	Jephson House Blackdown Leamington Spa CV32 6RE
Liverpool Housing Trust	Martin Rayson	12 Hanover Street Liverpool L1 4AA
London & Quadrant Housing Trust	Michael Yarde	Osborn House Osborn Terrace London SE3 9DR

Organisation	Contact name	Address
London Borough of Lewisham Council	Adrian Lewis	Lewisham Town Hall Catford London SE6 4RU
London Borough of Newham Council	Chris Wood	Town Hall Barking Road East Hame London E6 2RP
Metropolitan Housing Trust	Paul Clarke Chris Byrne	Cambridge House 109 Mayes Road Wood Green London N22 6UR
North London Muslim Housing Association	Saif Ahmad	62 Cazenove Road London N16 6BJ
Nottingham City Council	Neil Barks	The Guildhall Nottingham NG1 4BT
Pavilion Housing Association	Sara Gosnold	Gordon House Gordon Road Aldershot GU11 1LD
Poole Borough Council	Simon Hendy	Civic Centre Poole BH15 2RU
Sanctuary Housing Association	Lynette Boyles	Fergus House 127 Fergus Drive Glasgow G20 6BY
South Gloucestershire Council	Peter Hall	Oriel House 8 Castle Street Thornbury Bristol BS35 1HB
Swan Housing Group	Paul Durkin	Pilgrim House High Street Billericay Essex CM12 9XY
Taunton Deane Borough Council	David Harrison	The Deane House Belvedere Road Taunton Somerset TA1 1HE

Organisation	Contact name	Address
The Quest Trust	Simon Buxton	1 Belmont Landsdown Road Bath BA1 5DZ
Touchstone Housing Association	Stewart Ferguson	PO Box 160 Touchstone House Whitley Village Coventry CV3 4HZ
Vale Housing Association	Steve Russell	The Old Maltings Vineyard Abingdon Oxfordshire OX14 3UJ